Devotions for a

Sensational Life

Devotions for a Sensational Life

W PUBLISHING GROUP™

www.wpublishinggroup.com

A Division of Thomas Nelson, Inc.
www.ThomasNelson.com

Published in Nashville, Tennessee, by Thomas Nelson, Inc.

Compiled and edited by Elizabeth Kea

Unless otherwise noted, all Scripture is from THE NEW KING JAMES VERSION. Copyright © 1979, 1980, 1982, Thomas Nelson, Inc., Publishers.

Scripture quotations noted KJV are from THE KING JAMES VERSION of the Bible.

Scripture quotations noted TLB are from THE LIVING BIBLE, copyright © 1971. Used by permission of Tyndale House Publishers, Inc., Wheaton, Illinois 60189. All rights reserved.

Scripture quotations noted NIV are from the HOLY BIBLE: NEW INTERNA-TIONAL VERSION®. Copyright © 1973, 1978, 1984 by International Bible Society. Used by permission of Zondervan Publishing House. All rights reserved.

Scripture quotation noted NLT are from the *Holy Bible*, New Living Translation, copyright © 1996. Used by permission of Tyndale House Publishers, Inc., Wheaton, Illinois 60189. All rights reserved.

Scripture quotations noted RSV are from the REVISED STANDARD VERSION of the Bible. Copyright © 1946, 1952, 1971, 1973 by the Division of Christian Education of the National Council of the Churches of Christ in the U.S.A. Used by permission.

Library of Congress Cataloging-in-Publication Data

Devotions for a sensational life / [compiled and edited by Elizabeth Kea].
   p. cm.
   ISBN 0-7852-6525-2 (hc)
   ISBN 0-8499-4474-0 (sc)
   1. Women—Religious life. I. Kea, Elizabeth Bonner, 1976–
BV4844 .D48 2002
242'.643--dc21

2002002793

Printed in the United States of America
04 05 06 07 08 PHX 5 4 3 2 1

I have come that they may have life, and that they may have it more abundantly.

—JOHN 10:10

Contents

SENSATIONAL GRACE:

Refreshment for the Weary and Worn-Out

SENSATIONAL CELEBRATION:

Thoughts to Keep You Smiling and Living Positively

SENSATIONAL ENCOURAGEMENT:
Words of Comfort, Peace, and Hope

SENSATIONAL FAITH:
Wisdom and Guidance for the Journey

Sensational Purpose

Reminders of Who
(and Whose) You Are

Blessed Assurance

Therefore, brethren, having boldness to enter the Holiest by the blood of Jesus . . . let us draw near with a true heart in full assurance of faith.

—HEBREWS 10:19, 22

*B*lessed assurance, Jesus is mine!
O what a foretaste of glory divine!
Heir of salvation, purchase of God,
Born of His Spirit, washed in His blood.

This is my story, this is my song,
Praising my Savior, all the day long;
This is my story, this is my song,
Praising my Savior, all the day long.

Perfect submission, perfect delight,
Visions of rapture now burst on my sight;
Angels descending bring from above
Echoes of mercy, whispers of love.

Perfect submission, all is at rest
I in my Savior am happy and blest,
Watching and waiting, looking above,
Filled with His goodness, lost in His love.

—FANNY J. CROSBY

Seeing Yourself as God Does

Before I formed you in the womb I knew you . . .

—JEREMIAH 1:5

He chose us in Him before the foundation of the world, that we should be holy and without blame before Him in love, having predestined us to adoption as sons by Jesus Christ to Himself, according to the good pleasure of His will, to the praise of the glory of His grace, by which He made us accepted in the Beloved.

—EPHESIANS 1:4–6

We all want to be somebody. The truth is, God created each one of us to be somebody and no life is an accident or unwanted in His eyes. He has given us *each* a distinct purpose or calling. It is not humility to deny the Lord's extraordinary qualities in us, it's low self-esteem.

High self-esteem means seeing yourself as God sees you, and recognizing that you are a unique person in whom He has placed specific gifts, talents, and purpose unlike anyone else. Memorize this, cut it out, paste it on your hand, and say it aloud fifty times a day. Do whatever it takes to help you remember it. This is the absolute truth about you, whether you can see it or not and whether or not anyone *else* recognizes it.

I have learned to value myself as God values me by deliberately thanking Him for any positive things I see. "Thank You, Lord, that I am alive, that I can walk, that I can talk, that I am neat, that I love my children, that I know Jesus. Thank You, God, that You have made me to be a person of worth and purpose." As we praise God for specific things, we are inviting His presence to bring transformation.

—STORMIE OMARTIAN
Lord, I Want to Be Whole

Where Is Your Identity?

Therefore, if anyone is in Christ, he is a new creation; old things have passed away; behold, all things have become new.

—2 CORINTHIANS 5:17

One of the reasons we must know who we are, is to determine what we'll do. We can't do this backward. I can't rely on what I do to determine who I am, because if what I do is snatched away or if I fail at it, then I'll see myself as a loser. Michelle Kwan is a phenomenal ice skater, but what happens when she can no longer skate? She will struggle if her only identity is in being a skater. What about the Tiger Woodses, Michael Jordans, and beauty queens of the world? What happens when they can no longer do what they now do? Will they lose personal confidence? Will they be confused or depressed? What about you? Is your identity wrapped up in what you do?

God gives us an identity before He gives us a job to do. In the Old Testament we read that before Abram became the father of many nations, he was given a new identity. God changed his name from Abram to Abraham, which means "Father of many nations" (see Gen. 17). In the Book of Judges, God gave Gideon a new identity. Gideon saw himself as the least in his family and saw his family as being the weakest in the whole town (Judg. 6:15). Before God asked Gideon to build an army and defeat the Midianites, He called him a mighty man of valor. God gave Gideon a new identity.

As believers and followers of Christ, you and I have been given a new identity. We don't get our identity from our driver's license; most of the stuff on that is embellished anyway! We don't get our identity from our passport; that just tells us where we've been. We don't get our identity from school report cards; most of us are still dealing with the negative things some teachers said. We don't get our identity from a mirror; we just use that to put on makeup. You and I get our identity from our Creator. God tells us who we are. It's through His eyes and His Word that we get a true picture of who we are.

—HOLLY WAGNER
Dumb Things She Does,
Dumb Things He Does

You Are Loved

I am convinced that nothing can ever separate us from his love. Death can't, and life can't. The angels can't, and the demons can't. Our fears for today, our worries about tomorrow, and even the powers of hell can't keep God's love away. Whether we are high above the sky or in the deepest ocean, nothing in all creation will ever be able to separate us from the love of God that is revealed in Christ Jesus our Lord.

—ROMANS 8:38–39 NLT

On your journey to God's heart, it is critical that you know you are loved. You have the assurance of God that He will never leave you nor forsake you (Heb. 13:5). You need never feel "unloved" because His love is everlasting. Your confidence is based in the wonderful truth of that childhood song "Jesus Loves Me, This I Know, for the Bible Tells Me So." He has chosen to love you, and nothing can separate you from His love. His love heals, comforts, and corrects. His love draws you on the journey toward His heart.

Lord, Your immeasurable love is enough for me. Thank You that

Your love is not dependent on my performance or my physical char-
acteristics. Your love encompasses all of my life, and this gives me
great security. I would not choose any other destination. I know I am
looking in the right place for love—Your heart.

—CYNTHIA HEALD
A Woman's Journey to
the Heart of God

The Truth About Who You Are

Behold what manner of love the Father has bestowed on us, that we should be called children of God!

—1 JOHN 3:1

Surrendering to God the essence of who we are allows Him to whisper a secret to us. Like seeing your reflection for the first time, God will reveal to you the truth about who you are. Several years ago, God used a little book called *Life of the Beloved* by Henri Nouwen to whisper to me: "'You are the Beloved,' and all I hope is that you can hear these words as spoken to you with all the tenderness and force that love can hold. My only desire is to make these words reverberate in every corner of your being— 'You are the Beloved.'"

That, my sisters, is our deepest identity. We are loved passionately by God. And I don't know why. It is a mystery, and it must remain a mystery. To understand it is to dismiss it as we are prone to dismiss every other love in our lives. If we discovered that God loved us because we were smart, then we would try to do everything we could to be smarter so He would love us more. If we met someone smarter than we are, we would fall into despair. We couldn't believe God would love us if we weren't the smartest. So I don't think God will ever let us know the reason that He loves us as passionately as He does. I don't have a clue why God loves me. But I believe in the core of my being that He does. So I surrender to it. I stop fighting it. I cease trying to figure it out. I collapse on it.

Nothing can take His love from us. I can say that of no other love. God pursues us, courts us, and woos us to remind us. His love changes every day; it either intensifies, or my understanding of it grows, but I don't think it really matters which it is. He doesn't get tired of us, and He isn't frustrated by our moods or by our appearance. His love is all we have ever dreamed of. We are free to place the whole weight of our identity on Him. He will not lean, crumble, struggle, stagger, or falter in any way. His love is the answer to the questions of the culture. His embrace, the way to freedom. And His kiss, the most passionate we will ever know.

This love is why we were made.

—NICOLE JOHNSON
Fresh-Brewed Life

God's Message to You

As the Father loved Me, I also have loved you; abide in My love.

—JOHN 15:9

But God demonstrates His own love toward us, in that while we were still sinners, Christ died for us.

—ROMANS 5:8

*I*t was December 25, 1984, and there I was on Christmas morning, standing in the studio, the only person in the building other than a security guard and a news reporter. I was feeling very sorry for myself—all alone, no phone callers, no visitors, just me spinning carols and hymns on the turntables while big tears ran down my cheeks.

"Nobody loves me, Lord!" I said aloud in my most forlorn voice. "Nobody loves me!" I was sobbing by this point, feeling the most alone I'd ever felt in all my life. Then I heard his voice speaking to my heart as clearly and distinctly as the words on this page: "I love you, Liz. I love you."

My response was immediate and instinctive; I dropped to my

knees. What love is this, that he would speak to me, his child, on Christmas morning! At that moment, the words of the music blasting out of the studio speakers penetrated my heart: "Joy to the world! The Lord is come!"

He came to us then, he comes to us now, and his message is still the same: "Have no fear of the cold. I love you!"

—LIZ CURTIS HIGGS
Only Angels Can Wing It,
the Rest of Us Have to Practice

Longing for God

As the deer pants for the water brooks,
So pants my soul for You, O God.
My soul thirsts for God, for the living God.

—PSALM 42:1–2

Saint Augustine said that our souls will never find their rest until they find it in God. *He* is the treasure. Our longings will point the way to Him every single time. Each longing in my life that I have discovered, or that has discovered me, drives me to confront a truth that I might not have confronted otherwise: I need God. I am thirsty for God. Desperately thirsty. In every area of my life. I was made by Him and for Him, and apart from Him, I will not be satisfied. My desires for things to fill me and make me whole bear witness to the One who will fill me ultimately. My longing to be known reveals to me this existence of a greater knowing by the One who created me. My hunger for heaven gently sings to me a haunting lullaby that reminds me where we've come from and why we'll never feel fully at home here.

It is easy to miss this. Listen closely to your longings. I have veered off into sin and missed the treasure on many trips. Sin is trying to meet legitimate needs in an illegitimate way. Every sin that we choose to commit is tied to some very real need in our lives. We try to meet that need or longing with something or someone who cannot meet it. We say to God, "I don't trust You to take care of this situation, or fill this longing, so I will do it myself." We are fooled that the treasure is really the food, or the affair, not the living God . . .

Right now we can only see a dim reflection, but one day we will look into His eyes—the eyes that have seen from the foundation of the world . . . All of our hungers, all of our longings will melt in the power of His gaze when it meets ours. Everything we were created to be will be evident, and we will know as we are known. We will *feel* known by God. I can hardly imagine it. We will be whole, filled, and satisfied. All of our pain, every last ounce of our sorrow, any emptiness that we have felt will vanish like the morning dew. Gone. We will kneel in His presence in a place where there are no tears and where lions lie down with lambs. The intensity of His love and the encompassing of His embrace will overwhelm us. As our hearts finally receive all that we have longed for, I imagine some will dance, some will weep, but all of us will know we are home, at last.

—NICOLE JOHNSON
Fresh-Brewed Life

Receiving God's Love

Yes, I have loved you with an everlasting love;
Therefore with lovingkindness I have drawn you.
Again I will build you, and you shall be rebuilt.

—JEREMIAH 31:3–4

The key to receiving God's love is deciding to believe that it is there for you, and choosing to open up to it. Nothing can separate us from God's love except our own inability to receive it.

The Bible says, "The LORD's unfailing love surrounds the man who trusts in him" (Ps. 32:10 NIV). The more you say, "Okay, God, I'm going to trust Your promises and all You say about me and my circumstances and choose to believe You," the more you will experience God's love.

Receiving the gift of God's love means that we don't have to do desperate things for approval. Nor do we have to be depressed when we don't receive love from other people exactly the way we feel we need it. When we sense God's love, it takes the pressure off relationships and frees us to be who we were made to be . . .

Opening up and receiving God's love makes you more able to love others, even people for whom you have no natural affinity. Radiating love toward others is part of perfecting God's love in you. It also causes people to love *you* more. People who have the fullness of God's love flowing through them are always beautiful and attractive to those around them.

God's love is always more than we expect. That's why we are brought to tears so often in His presence. They are tears of gratitude for love beyond our imagination.

—STORMIE OMARTIAN
Finding Peace for
Your Heart

Inscribed on His Hands

Can a woman forget her nursing child,
And not have compassion on the son of her womb?
Surely they may forget,
Yet I will not forget you.
See, I have inscribed you on the palms of My hands.

—ISAIAH 49:15–16

One evening years ago, a woman came up to me after a presentation and cordially extended her hand. As I greeted her, I couldn't help noticing that clearly written on the palm of her hand were the letters, T-A-P-E.

What in the world was that all about? Maybe she was a warden, and it was a reminder to "Treat All Prisoners Equally." Maybe she was taking flying lessons and needed to remember to check "Time, Altitude, Pressure, Energy." I know! She's a waitress and that day's special desserts were "Tapioca, Apple pie, Peach cobbler, and Egg custard"!

My curious mind was on tilt as I debated, *Should I say something or not?* Finally, I couldn't stand it. "What do you mean, 'TAPE'?" I asked.

She looked at her hand, slapped her palm on her forehead, and moaned. "Even when I wrote it down, I forgot," she said, shaking her head. "Before I left the house tonight, I was supposed to start the VCR to tape a program for my kids!"

Oh. Never would have thought of that, and apparently, she didn't either. Our memories are not always what we want them to be, even when we write things down in the handiest places we can think of.

The good news is, God remembers to read his hand, and that's precisely where he has written your name. It isn't cheating for him to write it there, like it was for us in school. He does that for your sake, not his own. He can show you absolute proof: "See, I didn't forget you. Your name is right here on the palms of my hands." So personal, so visual, such an unforgettable image.

Those same palms would be pierced with nails on Calvary, leaving scars to prove once again that he has not forgotten you. "Reach your finger here," he said to the apostle Thomas, "and look at My hands . . . Do not be unbelieving, but be believing" (John 20:27).

—LIZ CURTIS HIGGS
Mirror, Mirror on the Wall,
Have I Got News for You!

It's About Who You Are

The Spirit Himself bears witness with our spirit that we are children of God, and if children, then heirs—heirs of God and joint heirs with Christ, if indeed we suffer with Him, that we may also be glorified together.

—ROMANS 8:16–17

S ometimes when asked, "Do you want to change the world?" women reply, "How on earth could I do that?" We are intimidated by the question; we think that changing the world is too big for us. That's better left to someone more talented or articulate. *How could I change the world? There is nothing remarkable in what I do. I raise kids, I drive the car pool; I'm not going to invent anything or influence anyone; I don't wear makeup to the grocery store; I can't even find my car keys . . . Change the world? You've got to be kidding!* But inside we know we want to . . .

Tim Keller, the senior minister at Redeemer Presbyterian in New York City, recently asked this question: "Did you buy in to Christianity to serve God or to have God serve you?" Are you willing to use what God has given you to radically impact this world? Or do you think it's better to stay calm, hide our gifts, and never rock the boat?

Not only is God calling us to rock the boat, He's calling us to get out of the boat! Each of us as women has a mandate on our life to make a difference in this world. Not because we're women, but because we're Christians. That difference at its core is not about what we do, but about who we are. I believe we are called to use our gifts to leave this world better than we found it: with more love, more forgiveness, more hope.

—NICOLE JOHNSON
Fresh-Brewed Life

Accepting Your Value

Nevertheless the solid foundation of God stands, having this seal:
"The Lord knows those who are His," and,
"Let everyone who names the name of Christ depart from iniquity.
—2 TIMOTHY 2:19

We are like onions . . . The onion begins at the core, and each and every layer builds upon the "onion-ness" inside. An authentic life and self is one in which the layers on the outside are merely expressions of the core on the inside.

The core on the inside is what we surrender to God. I tried to work my way from the outside of the onion in. Doing spiritual things, dressing a certain way, trying to be a submissive wife—all of those things are external things that don't define the core; they reflect the core. Our identity is not determined by these things.

For example, our dogs drink out of the toilet. I'm "oversharing" here, but there is a point to this. They eat out of a dog bowl, and they eliminate waste outdoors. Now, if tomorrow I began to drink out of the toilet and eat out of a dog bowl and go to the bathroom outside, would you think that I was a dog? You might think I was confused, but you would not think I was a dog. You would notice instantly the discrepancy between the inside core (human) and the outside behavior (dog).

What you do doesn't determine who you are in the core of your being, but it does reflect what you believe to be at the core of your being. No one acts inconsistently with who they see themselves to be. Remember Hans Christian Andersen's story of *The Ugly Duckling*? The duckling was bitten and made fun of for being so ugly. He was utterly miserable. He tried everything to be a better duck and to "fit in" with the animals in the barnyard. Then he saw his reflection. He wasn't a duck at all; he was a swan. A beautiful, graceful swan. Swans make terrible ducks, and even worse chickens, and if it were even possible, they wouldn't be very good cats. All of which the duckling tried to be. It wasn't until he discovered the core that the externals made sense. His inner identity changed his outer activity. It moved him from striving to resting. It changed him from trying to prove his worth to accepting his value. In short, he became a believer in the One who made him because he finally understood who he was.

—NICOLE JOHNSON
Fresh-Brewed Life

Being a Woman of Purpose

You will show me the path of life;
In Your presence is fullness of joy;
At Your right hand are pleasures forevermore.

—PSALM 16:11

*P*ursuing new experiences and achievements is exhilarating and healthy. But in each of the areas we've discussed there's the possibility of blind striving, an inability to see the limitations of that for which we strive. Many of us are slow to learn the obvious. We continually fall into the trap of thinking, *If I just had . . . I would be much more content.* Possession and life itself have meaning only when I come to terms with the God who created all things. When He is my foundation, the Being around whom my life revolves, only then will I have a sense of purpose. When that purpose becomes well defined, I recognize that everything I strive for is limited in its potential to produce fulfillment. That does not mean I can't, shouldn't, or won't seek . . . but it does mean I must realize that my ultimate joy will never come from things or persons. It will only come from a personal knowledge of and commitment to God.

In the midst of all his resplendent living, the writer of Ecclesiastes concludes: "I know that everything God does will remain forever; there is nothing to add to it and there is nothing to take from it" (3:14 NASB). The lack of permanence so common to the affairs of the heart directly contrasts with the longevity of the love we receive from God. We experience the joy that "would fill the earth and last till the end of time" only as we commune with the divine. "Everything God does will remain forever."

—MARILYN MEBERG
Choosing the Amusing

Just Because You're You

Do not be ashamed of the testimony of our Lord . . . who has saved us and called us with a holy calling, not according to our works, but according to His own purpose and grace which was given to us in Christ Jesus before time began.

—2 TIMOTHY 1:8–9

Women are often defined by their relationships—Bob's wife, Betty's mom, Helen's daughter, Mary's sister. And when you run out of family to make identifying associations, there is always your job, church affiliation, neighborhood, state, or size and appearance to define you—i.e. the pretty blonde who wears bright colors.

What tells *you* who you are? Sure, all these roles and associations help pinpoint a certain person. But how do you know who *you* are, beyond these descriptive phrases? In other words, how can you affirm yourself as a person with uniqueness, worth, and significance?

Some friends of mine enjoy tracking down their ancestors to determine a sense of identify. A good, solid pedigree can define a person for generations back.

When my children were young and I was known primarily as Chase's mom, or Jason's mom, or Sara's mom, I used to worry what would happen when they grew up and I no longer used that distinguishing label as frequently. Would I still be a real person? Or would I just disappear from the earth? Would I ever be known just by my own name? . . .

Ask some women who they are, and they will answer by telling you what they do professionally or where they work. And the bigger job they have to report, the more significant they feel.

To be successful and recognized by others helps a woman establish a sense of identity, it's true. In being noticed and loved by family, friends, and acquaintances, your self-esteem is nurtured. But there is more to who you are.

Totally apart from whom you are kin to, apart from your talents and gifts, apart from your employment and achievements, is the mature sense of identity that is *you*. Significantly, this is the *you* made in the image of God. This is the *you* that is loved by God for yourself alone. You are somebody because God loves you. You are special to God just because you're *you*—no other reason is needed. All these other relationships? Just icing on the cake.

—SUZANNE DALE EZELL
Living Simply in God's Abundance

Being Yourself

For you are all sons of God through faith in Christ Jesus . . . There is neither Jew nor Greek, there is neither slave nor free, there is neither male nor female; for you are all one in Christ Jesus. And if you are Christ's, then you are Abraham's seed, and heirs according to the promise.

—GALATIANS 3:26, 28–29

We are the most appealing to others, and the happiest within, when we are completely ourselves. But it is a constant struggle because, as Scripture teaches, the world is always trying to press us into its mold. The mold of the world is the mold of the synthetic, the mold of the artificial, the mold of the celluloid—the "Plastic Person."

The world cries, "You've got to be young and you've got to be tan. You've got to be thin and you've got to be rich. You've got to be great." But Scripture says, "You don't have to be any of those things. You simply have to be yourself—at any age—as God made you, available to Him so that He can work in and through you to bring about His kingdom and His glory." Now relax. Trust Him and be yourself. It certainly isn't easy, but it is possible.

Sometimes it is tough to be me because I don't like me. I'm disappointed in me. I'm embarrassed at the way I look, or I'm not being understood and affirmed by somebody I want to love me. Clearly, without doubt, there is nothing wrong with seeking to change within ourselves what is able to be changed (I am a strong advocate of that). But the essence of who we are—our age, our sex, our looks, our past, our shortcomings, our broken promises to ourselves, our unfulfilled dreams—we must learn to live with and to accept for what it is. We must seek to walk in God's light and in His counsel, realizing that contentment, acceptance, love, compassion, vulnerability, and charm are the by-products of an intimate relationship with Him, not the results of conforming to the mandates and demands of an insatiable world . . .

Simply put, it takes getting outside ourselves and creating what is not balanced and blended, with getting inside ourselves and accepting what is.

—LUCI SWINDOLL
You Bring the Confetti,
God Brings the Joy

We Are Opals, Not Diamonds

It is God who works in you both to will and to do good for His good pleasure.

—PHILIPPIANS 2:13

S he's a diamond in the rough" is a familiar way of saying somebody has potential to become far more than she is right now. But I believe that we are much more like opals than diamonds. Did you know that an opal is made of desert dust, sand, and silica and owes its beauty not to its perfection but to a defect? The opal is a stone with a broken heart. It is full of minute fissures that allow air inside, and then the air refracts the light. As a result, the opal has such lovely hues that the stone is called "the lamp of fire" because the breath of the Lord is in it.

An opal will lose its luster if it is kept in a cold, dark place, but the luster is restored when it is held in a warm hand or when light shines on it.

In so many ways, we can compare the opal to ourselves. It is when we are warmed by God's love that we take on color and brilliance. It is when we are broken inside ourselves—through our defects—that we can give back the lovely hues of His light to others. It is then that the lamp of the temple can burn brightly within us and not flicker or go out.

Without God's touch in our lives—His work in us to will and to do His good pleasure—there is no sparkle or scant joy. But when we allow Him to work within us—when we feel His hand upon us—we are no longer hidden treasures; we become sparkling jewels that beautify His kingdom.

—BARBARA JOHNSON
Splashes of Joy in the
Cesspools of Life

God Rejoices over You

Both the one who makes men holy and those who are made holy are of the same family. So Jesus is not ashamed to call them brothers. He says, "I will declare your name to my brothers; in the presence of the congregation I will sing your praises."

—HEBREWS 2:11–12 NIV

*B*ored Royal Air Force pilots stationed on the Falkland Islands devised what they thought was a wonderful game. Noting that the local penguins seemed fascinated by airplanes, the pilots searched out a beach where the greatest congregation of birds gathered. Then the pilots flew their planes slowly along the water's edge as nearly ten thousand penguins turned their heads in unison, watching the planes go by. When the pilots turned around to fly back, the birds turned their heads in the opposite direction, like spectators at a slow-motion tennis match. To give the penguins a little variety, the pilots flew out to sea, turned around, and flew over the top of the penguin colony. Once again, in unison, heads went up, up, up, until all ten thousand penguins toppled softly on their backs.

The simple zest for life that these darling, bowled-over birds personify is also expressed in my heart as I am reminded of God's presence within me as stated in Zephaniah 3:16–18:

Cheer up, don't be afraid. For the Lord your God has arrived to live among you. He is a mighty Savior. He will give you victory. He will rejoice over you in great gladness; he will love you and not accuse you." Is that a joyous choir I hear? No, it is the Lord himself exulting over you in happy song (TLB).

Can you imagine God's delight in us is so genuine, so spontaneous, so spirited that He exults over us by singing happy songs? Can you imagine that He not only lives among us (within us) and promises to give us victory, but also that He rejoices over us in great gladness? Who in your lifetime—past, present, or future—has ever been or will ever be so utterly in love with you?

Only God! Plain, simple, profound. That realization is enough to cause me to look up, up, up, and topple over with cheer-inducing, heartfelt gratitude.

—MARILYN MEBERG
I'd Rather Be Laughing

You Are God's Creation

For you are a holy people to the LORD your God, and the LORD has chosen you to be a people for Himself, a special treasure above all the peoples who are on the face of the earth.

—DEUTERONOMY 14:2

But we have this treasure in earthen vessels, that the excellence of the power may be of God and not of us.

—2 CORINTHIANS 4:7

*L*ife is holy. Our days, our hours, our minutes are holy, created by God according to His holy purpose. The Bible begins with a beautiful, poetic account of how and what God created. He made a special place. He made it self-contained and filled it with His wonders. Then He gave male and female dominion over it all.

God loved the world and all the creatures He put here. In fact, He loved it so much, He decided to come and dwell here, to walk among the people, to dwell in the countrysides and to visit the lakes and mountains. In Christ He reclaimed the world as a place of fulfillment and transcendence. God revealed Himself in the ordinary; He chose human life as His dwelling place. His presence and His purpose put us on holy ground.

What does that mean? *God is with us.* In the hubbub of our lives, God is with us—in the deadlines, in the splendor, in the singing of a bird, in the frustration of a broken relationship, in the sound of a little voice calling for Mom, in the plumbing repair, in a friend's phone call. He is there in it all; He is present with us. He opens doors for us to love one another, for us to experience peace and beauty. He opens doors for us to enjoy life, to laugh, to find ourselves, and to experience His very holiness, to experience the abundant life.

—SUZANNE DALE EZELL
*Living Simply in God's
Abundance*

Life in God

Then you will call upon Me and go and pray to Me, and I will listen to you.

—JEREMIAH 29:12

Look! I have been standing at the door and I am constantly knocking. If anyone hears me calling him and opens the door, I will come in and fellowship with him and he with me.

—REVELATION 3:20 TLB

$\mathcal{E}$very woman is on a journey searching for answers to her life. What is her purpose and why is she here? Life is more than the clothes a woman wears, the food she eats, the car she drives, the career she builds, the children she bears, or the house she lives in. When a woman searches for God and opens her heart's door, a miraculous thing happens. She discovers the dry, parched emptiness of her soul begins to fill with a divine dew. It's called the Spirit of God.

We are not unlike Jacob in the Old Testament who was alone

on a 400-mile journey. At one point, God spoke and said, "I am with you and will watch over you wherever you go" (Gen. 28:15). Jacob was not aware that God was already with him, just as we are not aware that God is already with us. He stands at the door of every woman's heart, calling her name, before she knows it.

—BARBARA JENKINS
Wit and Wisdom for Women

God Delights in You

As the bridegroom rejoices over the bride,
So shall your God rejoice over you.

—ISAIAH 62:5

I'm filled with wonder and cheer at the thought of how
delightfully God has created penguins. They charm me and
inspire me spiritually. They are waddling little overcomers who
because of a God-created system survive Earth's harshest environment, living out their quirky lives with efficiency as well as
organization. What's the source of their overcoming abilities?
God. Plain, simple, and profound.

I love that Jesus made references to the birds of the air and the
flowers of the field as objects of His loving care. In the divine
mind, all creation is valued and provided for. In fact, Jesus even
suggested we look to nature to note creation's God-given ability
to function, perform, and overcome, and then to be encouraged
and cheered that His commitment to meeting our needs is even
greater. What is equally inspiring to me is that God takes obvious

delight in His creation. (You have to admit, hatching an egg on the toe of a penguin is zany!)

God's delight in us is expressed frequently in Scripture. For example, Psalm 18:19 states, "He brought me out into a spacious place; he rescued me because he delighted in me." It's mind-boggling to most of us that the God of the universe actually delights in us, but Scripture says He does.

—MARILYN MEBERG
I'd Rather Be Laughing

Knowing Your Position

But you are a chosen generation, a royal priesthood, a holy nation,
His own special people, that you may proclaim the praises of Him
who called you out of darkness into His marvelous light.

—1 PETER 2:9

Today's woman cannot be defined. Tomorrow's woman, the woman of the twenty-first century, will be even more diverse. While some might describe her as harried, trying to balance conflicting roles, she is in fact invigorated by the challenge. The Christian woman finds vitality and stimulation instead of pressure and stress. She is a living paradox of peace stepping into unknown positions in her work, her family life, and her faith. She thrives on challenge.

This two-thousand-year-old definition is the best: She is chosen—and she knows her position.

She is one of a royal priesthood—with constant, direct communication with her Maker. There is never an indirect path or downtime when she cannot connect.

She belongs—she's part of a community beyond geography, beyond race, beyond special interests. Her community has no walls.

And she has a purpose—to be her Maker's advertisement and bring him applause.

—MIRIAM NEFF
Sisters of the Heart

Sensational Grace

～

Refreshment for the
Weary and Worn-Out

Is It for Me?

I live by faith in the Son of God, who loved me and gave Himself for me.

—GALATIANS 2:20

Is it for me, dear Savior,
Thy glory and Thy rest,
For me, so weak and sinful?
O shall I be so blessed?

O Savior, my Redeemer,
What can I but adore,
And magnify and praise Thee,
And love Thee evermore?

Is it for me, Thy welcome,
Thy gracious "Enter in,"
For me Thy "Come, ye blessed,"
For me so full of sin?

O Savior, precious Savior,
My heart is at Thy feet;
I bless Thee, and I love Thee,
And Thee I long to meet.

I'll be with Thee forever,
And never grieve Thee more;
Dear Savior, I must praise Thee,
And love Thee evermore.

—FRANCES RIDLEY HAVERGAL

You Need Carry No Baggage

There is therefore now no condemnation to those who are in Christ Jesus, who do not walk according to the flesh, but according to the Spirit. For the law of the Spirit of life in Christ Jesus has made me free from the law of sin and death.

—ROMANS 8:1–2

If we say that we have no sin, we deceive ourselves, and the truth is not in us. If we confess our sins, He is faithful and just to forgive us our sins and to cleanse us from all unrighteousness.

—1 JOHN 1:8–9

I am sometimes surprised at the things women feel bad about. We carry guilt over the junk we did in our preteen years, our teen years, and every year thereafter.

How can this be? If Jesus tells us he sings our praises, how can we drag through life shouldering guilt? Our Father says he forgave every wrong thing we ever did the moment his Son died for us. It's history, sister. We are positioned as sisters to Jesus, God's daughters; both Jesus and his Father find us delightful. Jesus sings about us.

May I illustrate from my experience as a little farm girl? Life reminds me of opening the sagging wooden gate and stepping into our delightful southern Indiana meadow. I was free to run. Running barefooted through soft clover, I went from dry earth to the soggy grasses near the pond. Cow pies dotted the meadow. I was made to run; God wired me that way. But I stepped in a lot of stuff on the way to the pond.

And then God washed my feet. They are clean.

I have seen women's postures change when they learned their position as God's daughter. When we know we're forgiven, we stand tall. No wonder. Remember, we need carry no baggage.

—MIRIAM NEFF
Sisters of the Heart

Freedom Through Christ

For by grace you have been saved through faith, and that not of your-
selves; it is the gift of God, not of works, lest anyone should boast.

—EPHESIANS 2:8–9

Trying to be perfect, wanting to please God, serving the body of Christ adequately—I often find that all these desires become blurred and I grow confused about how much or how little I must *do*. I don't always bridle my tongue; I rarely visit orphans and widows; I don't love impartially. I assume that I must try harder and do more to make up for my lack of obedience.

At this point Grace exclaims, "No! You now live in my realm of freedom, and you have the ever-present strength and help of the Holy Spirit. You must not try harder; you must strive less. You must acknowledge your helplessness and total dependence upon the Spirit for your guidance, your area of service, and your ability to love. You are created for good works, but they must flow out of your abiding communion with the living Vine."

Just as Mary of Bethany sat at the feet of Jesus listening to His words (while Martha was serving anxiously), Mary could not help but rise up and serve her Lord. It was her love for Jesus that moved her to abide in Him. As she abided, she was prompted to take her alabaster jar of perfume to anoint the Lord for burial—an incredible act of service that will always be told in remembrance of her.

True service always finds its source in loving our Savior, wanting to hear His Word, and then promptly obeying. As we listen to the Lord in faith with a willing heart, He can use us and produce His fruit in us. Our major work is to trust, abide, and obey. This is freedom from the law, and it is freedom to serve. My trust and faith in walking in the Spirit, and my love for the Lord, will assure my good works.

—CYNTHIA HEALD
Becoming a Woman of Grace

Giving Up and Waking Up

We have such trust through Christ toward God. Not that we are suf-
ficient of ourselves to think of anything as being from ourselves, but
our sufficiency is from God.

—2 CORINTHIANS 3:4–5

I have fallen asleep on God on more occasions than I can count. I have tried to memorize chapters of Scripture and found that I've killed so many brain cells trying to be thin and holy that I'm no longer able. I thought that Jesus said, "Come unto Me, all you who are weary and heavy laden, and I will give you more to *do* than anyone else!" But Jesus didn't say that. He promised me rest. But I couldn't find it. My constant struggle to be "godly" left me tired, empty, lonely on the inside, and ready to give up . . .

I had worked for God and yet withheld my heart from Him. I'd sought to please Him, like a father who is hard to please, and missed that He was pleased with me. I tried to do so many things *for* God that I missed being *with* God. Where was the goodness in that? I was the keeper of the covenant. I was the one making the sacrifice. I thought what Jesus did for me paled in comparison to what I was doing for Him! God was so pleased to see me surrender, He probably laughed. I think He got tired just watching me. I discovered that the Christian life is not about trying harder. It is not about keeping it all together. It is about trusting in the One who can keep it all together. Martin Luther said that we show whether or not we believe the gospel by what we do when we sin. If we just roll up our sleeves and try harder, we are not walking with Jesus. If we can do it all ourselves, what do we need Him for?

When I gave up, I began to wake up. I felt the gentle stirring in my soul to respond to God. He whispered to me, "Jesus came to give you life." *Life? What is life if it isn't running all the time?* Peace—real peace on the inside, from all of this climbing, striving, and worrying. Joy—unabashed delight in life, regardless of the circumstances. Love—foundational, unconditional, never-ending love. I didn't have to work for these things, I just had to surrender to them. I had to stop long enough to let them overtake me. Again and again.

—NICOLE JOHNSON
Fresh-Brewed Life

Everything Through
God's Strength

Therefore, having been justified by faith, we have peace with God through our Lord Jesus Christ, through whom also we have access by faith into this grace in which we stand, and rejoice in hope of the glory of God.

—ROMANS 5:1–2

I can't do it!" I cried to God in prayer shortly after Michael and I were married. "I can't handle the dishes—I can't handle the house—I can't handle my work-I can't handle the loneliness of being a wife of someone who works all the time—I can't deal with my own emotional ups and downs, let alone his! I can't do any of it, God, not any of it." I wept before the Lord with a mixture of frustration and guilt over the fact that I was feeling this way about my husband, my home, and my life. God had rescued me from the pit of hell and death just three years before and had given me hope and a future. How could I—who knew what it was to be hungry and poor and feel there was no love or purpose in my life—tell God I couldn't handle these answers to my prayers?

Fortunately, the Lord did not strike me with lightning; instead He waited quietly until I was finished and then softly reminded me, *You are trying to do everything in your own strength.* As I sat there in my discouragement, I sensed the Holy Spirit speaking to my heart saying simply, *All you have to do is worship Me in the midst of what you are facing and I will do the rest.*

"Oh, thank You, Lord," I prayed through my tears. "I think I can at least handle doing that much."

I lifted my hands and said out loud, "Lord, I praise You in the midst of my situation. Thank You that You are all powerful and there is nothing too hard for You. Thank You for who You are and all You have done for me. I worship You, Jesus, Almighty God, Holy Father, Lord of my life." As I continued to praise and thank God for all that He is, that hopelessly out-of-control feeling diminished.

"Lord, I give You my home, my marriage, my husband, and my work. They are Yours," I said as my shoulders relaxed, the knot in my stomach left, and I sighed with tears of relief. The pressure was off. The burden now was *His.* I didn't have to try to be perfect anymore, and I didn't have to beat myself up when I wasn't.

Since that time, praise has become a habitual attitude of my heart that says, "No matter what is going on in and around me, *God is in charge!* I trust Him to bring good out of this situation and work things out for my highest blessing."

Praise is not always my first reaction to things, so I often have to remind myself of Pastor Jack Hayford's teaching on praise: "It's not your saying, 'I'll give it everything I've got and the Lord will bless it,' but rather it's the Lord saying to you, 'You just bless My name and *I'll* give it everything *I* have.'" Now, when I come to the place where my flesh can't go any further, I stop where I am and worship God. This key has unlocked even the heaviest of closet doors and illuminates the darkest of nights.

—STORMIE OMARTIAN
Finding Peace for Your Heart

Grace Is God

But He was wounded for our transgressions,
He was bruised for our iniquities;
The chastisement for our peace was upon Him,
And by His stripes we are healed.
All we like sheep have gone astray;
We have turned, every one, to his own way;
And the LORD has laid on Him the iniquity of us all.

—ISAIAH 53:5–6

*G*race is one of those "theological" words that we say we believe in and even count on, but sometimes it's good to consider what grace really *does* mean in a world where the gloomees are always out to get you. As Lewis Smedes says, "God's grace can make life all RIGHT despite the fact that everything is obviously all WRONG . . . Grace is the reality of God entering history—and our lives—to make things right at the very center."

Grace does not stand for an escape mechanism, some kind of all-expense-paid trip to Disneyland because God knows we can't afford to go ourselves. Grace has nothing to do with Disneylands, Fantasy Islands, magical cures, or instant solutions.

You may have seen the acrostic on grace that puts it in perspective:

God's
Riches
At
Christ's
Expense

Jesus never used the word *grace*. God left that for Paul, but if you want to describe grace in one word it is *Jesus*.

Grace (Jesus) is the answer for our guilt and failure.

Grace (Jesus) is the strength we need to cope with life.

Grace (Jesus) is the promise that gives us the hope that keeps us going.

—BARBARA JOHNSON
Pack Up Your Gloomees in a
Great Big Box Then Sit on the
Lid and Laugh

The Source of Your Strength

For it pleased the Father that in Him all the fullness should dwell,
and by Him to reconcile all things to Himself, by Him, whether
things on earth or things in heaven, having made peace through the
blood of His cross.

—COLOSSIANS 1:19–20

I have coined my own definition of *perfectionism:* "a neurotic,
destructive syndrome designed to make you feel guilty when you
don't do what you think everybody else in the world wants you
to do." From personal experience I have found that true perfec-
tionists are pains in the neck. They never live up to their stan-
dards, but neither does anyone else. When they make a mistake,
it follows them around like a dark cloud . . .

The Bible says that "Noah was a just man, perfect in his generations. Noah walked with God" (Gen. 6:9). My *Strong's
Concordance* translates *perfect* in this passage as "complete, full,
undefiled, upright, full of integrity and truth." In Genesis 17:1
(KJV), God talked to Abram: "And when Abram was ninety years

old and nine, the LORD appeared to Abram, and said unto him, I am the Almighty God; walk before me, and be thou perfect." *Perfect* has the same meaning for Abram as it did for Noah. In Psalm 37:37 (KJV) are these words: "Mark the perfect man, and behold the upright: for the end of that man is peace." *Perfect* in this passage means "complete, pious, gentle, and dear." And where Jesus told us in Matthew to be perfect like our Father, He meant for us to be complete, full grown, and mature . . .

It's reassuring to me to know that only Jesus Christ was a perfect human being. And because He made the perfect sacrifice for me, I can become perfect (complete) in Him. I have nothing to prove.

Next time you get down on yourself because you can't do all things perfectly, don't beat yourself up. Don't blame other people. Don't keep striving for the impossible. Realize that perfectionism is a sickness; Jesus is the Redeemer. Look to the Source of your strength. You will never be able to be everything you should be. Only Jesus can supply that kind of completeness. Rest in Him.

—THELMA WELLS
What's Going On, Lord?

Coming to the Throne of Grace

And He said to me, "My grace is sufficient for you, for My strength is made perfect in weakness." Therefore most gladly I will rather boast in my infirmities, that the power of Christ may rest upon me.

—2 CORINTHIANS 12:9

I don't know how many times in my life I have said, "Lord, I can't do this." Each time the Lord has patiently replied, *I know you can't, Cynthia. But I can through you.* And that is the mystery and the good news of the sufficiency of His grace in our lives. And it is the comfort of knowing that God delights in working through those who are weak, inadequate, and unworthy. For His strength is made perfect in our weakness, His Spirit is our adequacy, and Christ in us makes us worthy.

Paul gave Timothy the admonition, "You therefore, my son, be strong in the grace that is in Christ Jesus" (2 Tim. 2:1 NASB). Our strength is in His grace and His grace alone. It is not in our abilities, in our accomplishments past or present, in our successful service, or in our praise and emulation of others. To be strong in His grace, we must learn to take hold of it and appropriate it for our needs.

Hebrews 4:15–16 teaches us how to take hold of God's grace with this encouragement: "This High Priest of ours understands our weaknesses, for he faced all of the same temptations we do, yet he did not sin. So let us come boldly to the throne of our gracious God. There we will receive his mercy, and we will find grace to help us when we need it"(NLT).

To be strong in His grace, *we must come to the throne of grace.* When Paul agonized over his thorn, he didn't go off in a corner to complain. He went to the Lord with his need and prayed for the thorn to be removed.

—CYNTHIA HEALD
A Woman's Journey to the Heart of God

Reject the Pitfall of Perfectionism

If you confess with your mouth the Lord Jesus and believe in your heart that God has raised Him from the dead, you will be saved.

—ROMANS 10:9

And she will bring forth a Son, and you shall call His name JESUS, for He will save His people from their sins.

—MATTHEW 1:21

One day my six-year-old daughter, knowing how much I love flowers, picked roses for me from our backyard. While she was getting my favorite vase down from the shelf, she dropped it on the tile floor, and it smashed into a hundred pieces. She was devastated and so was I, but I didn't punish her because I recognized her *heart* was perfect, even though her *performance* was *not*. She was doing what she did out of love, even though she was not able to accomplish it perfectly. The perfection God expects from us is just that. A heart that is pure in love toward God is a heart that desires to obey Him.

God knows our actions can never be 100 percent perfect. That's why He sent Jesus. Through Christ, He has given us access to the perfection only God can provide. Our hearts can be perfect even if our actions are not . . .

In our flesh we strive to succeed. We feel we're worth something when we win, worthless when we lose. What we demand of ourselves is always limited by the outer layer. Human perfection can only be as good as that. But God says He wants to make you something *more* than your human excellence. You will rise to the level and degree you sense His love in your life . . . I don't have to worry about being perfect because the perfection of Christ is manifested by His love flowing through me.

When you look in the mirror and see the excellence of Jesus reflected back, that's when you will have a sense of your true worth. The actual transformation takes place as you worship the Lord in and for *His* perfection.

—STORMIE OMARTIAN
Finding Peace for Your Heart

Not as We Deserve

Through the LORD's mercies we are not consumed,
Because His compassions fail not.
They are new every morning;
Great is Your faithfulness.
"The LORD is my portion," says my soul,
"Therefore I hope in Him!"

—LAMENTATIONS 3:22–24

I've spent fifteen years learning to understand what was accomplished on the cross, and it simply means that Jesus took all that I have coming to me—pain, failure, confusion, hatred, rejection, and death—and gave me all that He had coming to Him—all His wholeness, healing, love, acceptance, peace, joy, and life. Because of God's grace, all we have to do is say, "Jesus, come live in me and be Lord over my life."

Grace and mercy are much alike. Grace happens when God refrains from punishing a person who is guilty. Mercy is God's compassion for our misery beyond what may be expected. We need both.

If it weren't for God's grace *and* mercy, we wouldn't even be saved for the Bible tells us, "by *grace* you have been saved" (Eph. 2:8) and "accounting to His mercy He saved us" (Titus 3:5). Before we met Jesus we were "guilty" and "miserable," but His "grace" and "mercy" have saved us.

Grace has to do with it all being *Him. He* does it. Not us. Grace is always a surprise. You think it's not going to happen, and it does. Pastor Jack Hayford teaches about grace that "When the humble say, 'I don't have it and I can't get it on my own,' God says, 'I've got it and I'm going to give it to you.' That's God's grace."

—STORMIE OMARTIAN
Finding Peace for Your Heart

Easier Yokes and Lighter Burdens

Take My yoke upon you and learn from Me, for I am gentle and lowly in heart, and you will find rest for your souls. For My yoke is easy and My burden is light.

—MATTHEW 11:29–30

Jesus wants us to slow down, find rest, release our burdens. We are moving way outside my area of giftedness here.

He is saying, "Relax," and all I seem to excel in is running off in yet another direction. My husband would agree with him: "No new projects!" he insists, as I wildly outline some urgent new idea . . .

Prayer seems the logical path to these gentle words of Jesus beckoning us toward easier yolks and lighter burdens. The key, however, is in *sharing* our burdens with Christ, and in yoking ourselves to him so that we walk with him rather than against him.

This sounds good in theory, yet it's tough for me to do in real life. Instead of praying, "Lord, thy will be done," it comes out more like, "Lord, *my* will be done, and the sooner the better!"

Instead of prayerfully beginning my day by seeking his will, I sometimes (too often) find myself calling out for help at every inconvenience as I barrel along on my own agenda.

Sometimes I use prayers like a magic incantation, waving them over a situation like a wand, instead of desiring God's will for that moment. Flying off to a presentation, I pray (beg?) for the plane to land on schedule, when it might be more appropriate to pray for a calm spirit of resourcefulness, no matter what time it lands. On school mornings, when I run around the kitchen like a crazy woman trying to pack lunches and sign permission slips, I pray for help finding the children's library books, when a simple prayer for peaceful preparation the night before might have been a better move. Bill says I go through each day as if I'll never hit a red light. What he doesn't know is, I pray for green traffic lights too!

When I pray, "Lighten my load, Lord," the Lord's response is, "Take my yoke upon you and learn from me." Wait a minute . . . take on more? No, take on a partner. By yoking myself with him, my steps, by necessity, will become more "grace-full" as I learn how to follow his lead.

—LIZ CURTIS HIGGS
Mirror, Mirror on the Wall,
Have I Got News for You!

Abiding in God

LORD, my heart is not proud;
  my eyes are not haughty.
I don't concern myself with matters too great
  or awesome for me.
But I have stilled and quieted myself,
  just as a small child is quiet with its mother.
  Yes, like a small child is my soul within me.
O Israel, put your hope in the Lord—
  now and always.

—PSALM 131 NLT

I don't know about you, but I find more often than not that the high point of my day is going to bed at night! I've wondered if there's a message in there for me, but many times I am busy because I need to be and there's no good way around it. The other night as I fell thankfully into bed, I thought about a T-shirt I'd seen with the saying, "I am woman. I am invincible. I am tired." I know that many other women join me in feeling the need to experience the Lord's rest while we continue on His journey . . .

Rest, refreshment, and *renewal* are healing words. God wants to make them a reality in your life. The Lord Himself will provide everything you need, particularly rest and strength, for your daily walk. Green meadows and peaceful streams are part of your journey. Wear His yoke so that you allow Him to lead you there. Let Him set your pace and guide you to the right paths. Receive the freedom He offers you from having to worry about what lies ahead. Truly, the heart that accepts His will and guidance asks nothing. Abiding in Him provides the relationship that is the source of rest, discernment for service, strength, and the patience to wait and trust.

—CYNTHIA HEALD
A Woman's Journey to the Heart of God

The End of the Quest

So now, brethren, I commend you to God and to the word of His grace, which is able to build you up and give you an inheritance among all those who are sanctified.

—ACTS 20:32

*F*or years I felt a trifle guilty that I had an "it" quest. In fact, for years I wouldn't even admit I yearned for "it." I would berate myself for wanting more of whatever and not even know what the "whatever" was . . .

But what really put me in a slump was Deuteronomy 4:29: "But if . . . you seek the LORD your God, you will find him if you look for him with all your heart and with all your soul."

I blamed myself for not seeking Him hard enough. Then I'd think, *Maybe we should be in a different church, or maybe I need to pray longer, read Scripture more extensively, or maybe I need a different translation.* More damaging than these thoughts was the idea that *Maybe I'm not good enough, and the "it" is for others but not for me.*

Incidentally, that last thought came directly from the enemy. Anytime we feel diminished or accused of being unworthy, those are Satan's words. Jesus said in Revelation 12:10 that Satan is "the accuser of our brethren" (KJV). We can recognize his creepy voice anytime we feel accused. The Holy Spirit woos us, loves us, and moves us to a place of understanding. He never undermines us, His children, with derogatory messages that make us feel worthless. We are worth the price of Jesus on the cross, which makes us acceptable to a holy God just as we are. (That truth always makes me want to break into a joyful jig!)

I've learned that I must not quit seeking, that my rest will not be found anywhere but in Him, and that He fills me with His righteousness. I simply must realize that His supply is inexhaustible, and I will never plumb its depths. I can continue to seek, always with the happy knowledge that there is more, and it is not being withheld. That thought is then balanced with the realization that in heaven, finally, all will be told to me, experienced by me, and the "it" will be perfectly satisfied. In the meantime, I can relax, quit feeling guilty, enjoy the satisfactions He brings my way on earth, and recognize the best is yet to come.

—MARILYN MEBERG
I'd Rather Be Laughing

Sensational Celebration

~

Thoughts to Keep You
Smiling and Living Positively

Praise Him, Praise Him

But I have trusted in Your mercy;

My heart shall rejoice in Your salvation.

I will sing to the LORD,

Because He has dealt bountifully with me.

—PSALM 13:5–6

Praise Him! Praise Him! Jesus, our blessed Redeemer!

Sing, O Earth, His wonderful love proclaim!

Hail Him! hail Him! highest archangels in glory;

Strength and Honor give to His holy Name!

Like a shepherd, Jesus will guard His children,

In His arms He carries them all day long:

Praise Him! Praise Him!

Tell of His excellent greatness.

Praise Him! Praise Him!

Ever in joyful song!

Praise Him! Praise Him! Jesus, our blessed Redeemer!
For our sins He suffered, and bled, and died.
He our Rock, or hope of eternal salvation,
Hail Him! hail Him! Jesus the Crucified.
Sound His praises! Jesus who bore our sorrows,
Love unbounded, wonderful, deep and strong.

Praise Him! Praise Him! Jesus, our blessed Redeemer!
Heav'nly portals loud with hosannas ring!
Jesus, Savior, reigneth forever and ever.
Crown Him! Crown Him! Prophet, and Priest, and King!
Christ is coming! over the world victorious,
Pow'r and glory unto the Lord belong.

—FANNY J. CROSBY

Celebrating God

My heart is steadfast, O God,
  my heart is steadfast!
I will sing and make melody!
  Awake, my soul!
Awake, O harp and lyre!
  I will awake the dawn!
I will give thanks to thee, O Lord, among the peoples;
  I will sing praises to thee among the nations.
For thy steadfast love is great to the heavens,
  thy faithfulness to the clouds.
Be exalted, O God, above the heavens!
  Let thy glory be over all the earth!

—PSALM 57:7–11 RSV

The wisdom and doctrine of Scripture teach that the experience of celebrating God is the core of worship. It is the quintessence of praise and thanksgiving—the most perfect manifestation of a heart that gratefully fellowships with the One who provides life and all the gifts of living. In fact, a grateful heart is not only the greatest virtue, it is the seed bed for all other virtues. When we are caught up in the celebration of God there is neither room nor time for the invasion of negative living. As we rejoice before the Lord, as we serve Him in the area of our calling, as we enter joyfully into our daily journey, as we give thanks to Him for His kindness and faithfulness, we celebrate God.

Counting our blessings gives birth to that celebration. It cannot fail. In the words of Christina Rossetti:

Were there no God, we would be in this glorious world
with grateful hearts: and no one to thank!

—LUCI SWINDOLL
You Bring the Confetti,
God Brings the Joy

A Thankful Heart
Is a Happy Heart

Be glad in the LORD *and rejoice, you righteous;*
And shout for joy, all you upright in heart!

—PSALM 32:11

Blessed be the God and Father of our Lord Jesus Christ, who has blessed us with every spiritual blessing in the heavenly places in Christ.

—EPHESIANS 1:3

Being thankful is like an analogy I once read that talks of being given a dish of sand and being told there were particles of iron in it. We could look for the iron by sifting our clumsy fingers through the sand, but we wouldn't find much. If we took a magnet, however, and pulled it through the sand, it would draw to itself the almost invisible iron particles. The unthankful heart, like the clumsy fingers, discovers no mercies, but let the thankful heart sweep through the day, and as the magnet finds the iron, so will the thankful heart find heavenly blessings every time!

—BARBARA JOHNSON
Mama, Get the Hammer,
There's a Fly on Papa's Head!

Whatsoever Lovely

And in that day you will say:
"Praise the LORD, call upon His name;
Declare His deeds among the peoples,
Make mention that His name is exalted.
Sing to the LORD,
For He has done excellent things;
This is known in all the earth.

—ISAIAH 12:4–5

$\mathcal{T}$he Bible clearly provides the guidelines for achieving healthy thinking patterns. Paul said in Philippians 4:8, "Whatsoever things are true, whatsoever things are honest, whatsoever things are just, whatsoever things are pure, whatsoever things are lovely, whatsoever things are of good report, if there be any virtue, and if there be any praise, think on these things" (KJV). I believe Paul was encouraging us to make a choice in how we think. Once we make that choice we won't be victims of unhealthy thought patterns. Paul then delineated what would be good for us to think about.

I've always had a particular affinity for the message of that verse because of the way it became part of my childhood experience. My father pastored small rural churches in the state of Washington, and it was his custom to visit his church members' homes at least once every two weeks. Generally, these people lived on farms scattered around the little town of Amboy. To call on just two families often took an entire afternoon.

One of my favorite pastoral calls was to Mr. and Mrs. Wheeler's farm. Mrs. Wheeler was the most pleasant, jolly, and "laughy" lady I've ever known. She was exceedingly heavy and, not surprisingly, a fabulous cook. Her husband, who was not as tall as she and weighed at least one hundred pounds less, called her his "Baby Dumpling." She called him "Mr. Wheeler." They had been married for more than fifty years but spoke to each other with the tenderness of newlyweds. I loved being around them.

Mrs. Wheeler (I wouldn't dare call her Baby Dumpling, even behind her back) habitually interspersed her conversation with the phrase, "I was just thinking whatsoever lovely . . ." For example, she would respond to our noisy entrance onto their property with, "Well, Pastor, I was just thinking whatsoever lovely, and here you are!" or "I was just thinking whatsoever lovely when I decided to make a peach cobbler," or "I was just thinking whatsoever lovely when Mr. Wheeler surprised me with a kiss on the back of my neck."

These statements always seemed to inspire wonderfully contagious moments of laughter from Mrs. Wheeler. It was impossible not to join in, even when nothing about her comments seemed especially funny to me.

Lurching home from the Wheelers' one afternoon, I asked Dad why Mrs. Wheeler said "whatsoever lovely" about so many things. Dad was thoughtful for a minute and then replied, "Well, Marilyn, Mrs. Wheeler has a habit. She told me one time she could either think sad thoughts or glad thoughts, and she would rather think glad ones, or, as Scripture says, 'lovely' ones."

It wasn't that Mrs. Wheeler couldn't think of any sad thoughts to consider. I learned some years later that the Wheelers' only child had died of rheumatic fever at the age of six. Apparently, they had made a conscious choice about how they would cope with their loss. They chose "glad" over "sad," and they and those around them were the richer as a result of that choice.

—MARILYN MEBERG
I'd Rather Be Laughing

Celebrating Beauty

Oh, taste and see that the LORD is good;
Blessed is the man who trusts in Him!
Oh, fear the LORD, you His saints!
There is no want to those who fear Him.
The young lions lack and suffer hunger;
But those who seek the LORD shall not lack any good thing.

—PSALM 34:8–10

*B*oth my general and personal pursuits have been a constant effort to find the clearest expression of what I thought was beautiful in any chosen medium or avenue of communication . . . I have consciously sought after those things which make for value, order, richness, spirit, and wonder, even though I am often unable to verbalize what I feel when I perceive something beautiful. Sometimes it's a pang or a sensation; at other times it is an awareness of joy and security or pure pleasure. In any event, it is a moment to be celebrated. Beauty justifies itself. The fact that it defies definition means nothing . . .

Perhaps when we identify the distinguishing components of beauty, we will realize there are countless moments during the day to celebrate it, to praise God, to recognize that our world of factories and stock reports and guns and monotony is also a world filled with poetry, flowers, and light—beauty. Beauty brings magic and joy as it transforms and transfigures. It may last only a fleeting moment, but in that impermanence itself, beauty derives part of its enhancement. We must train ourselves to capture that passing moment of magic as our own.

When a sudden ray of sun or a moonbeam falls on a dreary street, it makes no difference what it illumines—a broken bottle on the ground, a fading flower in a field, or the flaxen blonde hair of a child's head. The object is transformed and the viewer is transfixed. Celebrate that moment of beauty and take it with you in your memory. It is God's gift to you.

—LUCI SWINDOLL
You Bring the Confetti,
God Brings the Joy

Celebrating Joy

Many, O LORD my God, are Your wonderful works
Which You have done;
And Your thoughts toward us
Cannot be recounted to You in order;
If I would declare and speak of them,
They are more than can be numbered.

—PSALM 40:5

*I*t is interesting that Jesus said it is impossible to enter the Kingdom unless we become as little children (Mark 10:15). I believe he recognized the need for adults to be jolted out of their dull, wooden mind-sets and assume the trusting unpretentiousness so characteristic of a child. Jesus placed a very high premium upon that childlike quality. The most profound truth in the universe is that God loves me; yet many miss that truth because of its simplicity. When Jesus said, "I praise thee, O Father, Lord of heaven and earth, that Thou didst hide these things from the wise and intelligent and didst reveal them to babes" (Matthew 11:25), he once again reminds us of how preferable it is at times to be childlike . . .

The expression of our child-spirit is not limited to our play instincts. It is also in an enjoyment and appreciation of the simple things in life. I call this my "shoestring" philosophy. I developed this perspective when I was four years old. My father had just administered a spanking meant to cure me of my wicked ways. At the conclusion of that discipline, Dad asked me what I thought about my spanking. My response to him was to announce that I didn't care because I had new shoestrings. (They had been purchased for me the day before.) One must admit there is something pathetic about a child whose only comfort for the moment is a pair of new shoestrings. Nonetheless, a bit of wisdom is found here. You have probably noticed that a child is frequently much more content with a simple toy than one that is elaborate in its many mechanical capabilities.

What are [your] tiny joys? . . . For me there is always that which appeals to my senses. There are certain smells which invariably put me into orbit: fresh cut grass, lilacs in the spring, roses, the earth after a rain, mountain air, fresh baked bread, Ken's aftershave. On the more peculiar side, I love the smell of gasoline, new rubber tires, basements, and—can you believe?—the mortar between bricks or stones. We have a large stone fireplace in our home and rare is the day I don't press my nose to the mortar and inhale ecstatically; it's especially rewarding just prior to or during a rain! (I can't believe I'm admitting to that peculiarity in print!) Then there is the joy of seeing the glory of nature—the sky, a tree, the ocean, a flower, the Colorado Rocky Mountains. There is the joy of feeling the smoothness of pebbles washed clean by the repeated pounding of the surf; the velvet softness of our cocker spaniel; the coolness of satin sheets against bare skin; of the coarseness or corduroy between the fingers.

After we have whittled away some of the deadwood of conventionality, we can investigate those little joys and those unrestrained experiences that may bring a smile to our lips.

You'll be amazed at the readiness with which you begin to laugh—and the frequency.

—MARILYN MEBERG
Choosing the Amusing

Putting on the Garment of Praise

A merry heart does good, like medicine,
But a broken spirit dries the bones.

—PROVERBS 17:22

*O*pportunities come in all shapes and sizes. What if those things you see now as obstacles could be seen instead as GOLD BRICKS? Bricks can be used to build a wall or as paving stones for your road to success. You can follow the yellow brick road to where you want to be, or you can remain stymied by that big wall that seals off any progress you want to make. *It all depends on how you look at the obstacles.*

You may have seen one of those drawings where the instructions ask you if you see a young girl or an old woman. If you look at the drawing one way, you will see a young girl. Look at it from a little different angle, and you will see an old woman.

The point is that perspective is all about how we choose to see things. Because we look as much with our mind as with our eyes, we tend to "see" what we expect to see or want to see. Changing our perspective calls for a *willingness to see things differently*. That's the key to developing a positive attitude regardless of what happens to us . . .

When problems suddenly hit you like a tornado, it does no good to deny the seriousness of the situation. What I'm talking about is developing a *positive, God-centered approach to life* that takes the good and the bad as it comes while putting on the garment of praise instead of a spirit of despair (Isa. 61:3 TLB).

Developing a positive attitude means working continually to find what is uplifting and encouraging. It can be done; I know because I've made a study of being positive.

—BARBARA JOHNSON
*Mama, Get the Hammer,
There's a Fly on Papa's Head!*

Changing Our Perspective

Behold, God will not cast away the blameless,
Nor will He uphold the evildoers.
He will yet fill your mouth with laughing,
And your lips with rejoicing.

—JOB 8:20–21

The ability to laugh over those unexpected and unwanted experiences that threaten to get the best of us enables us to change our perspective. Putting this philosophy into practice means that when something goes wrong, instead of being victimized by it, we lighten up, take the situation less seriously, and see if there isn't a laugh to be found somewhere. When we are able to do this, we are in control of our situation instead of our situation being in control of us . . .

You may feel there are times in life that simply will not yield even an ounce of humor. May I suggest that during those seemingly interminable times of pain, you fight to see beyond the restrictive confines of the immediate; remind yourself that those moments will not last forever. Whatever it is that threatens to crush your spirit and claim your joy today will not necessarily be there tomorrow, next month, or next year. Life moves forward and circumstances change. You will not always be in a pit! That reminder in itself brings a respite to the soul. From there perhaps a glimmer of light can seep through the darkness, enabling you to search out that seemingly elusive but spirit-lifting smile or laugh that helps you regain control.

—MARILYN MEBERG
Choosing the Amusing

Holy Humor

Then our mouth was filled with laughter,
And our tongue with singing.
Then they said among the nations,
"The LORD has done great things for them."
The LORD has done great things for us,
And we are glad.

—PSALM 126:2–3

I have a soft place in my heart for the good old days of television: of watching Carol Burnett transform herself into a washer woman, of watching Jack Benny fold his arms just so, of hearing Red Skelton, a man who once said, "If I can make people smile, then I have served my purpose for God," end his show by whispering "God bless." We can still watch Dick Van Dyke fall over the ottoman on late night reruns, but I miss the variety shows, the live television comedy hours, even the early years of *Saturday Night Live* . . .

Reinhold Niebuhr, best known for penning the Serenity Prayer, also wrote: "Humor is a prelude to faith, and laughter is the beginning of prayer." For those who love God, laughter isn't optional, it's scriptural. As we all love to repeat, "A merry heart does good like medicine" (Prov. 17:22). As a woman who believes in the power of faith *and* humor, I am heaven-bent on bringing more laughter into our lives.

Joy shows up in the Bible more than two hundred times, but I wish there were more in there about laughter. After all, we know "Jesus wept" (John 11:35). Why not another nice, short verse to assure us, "Jesus laughed"? Cal Samra, founder of the Fellowship of Merry Christians, of which I'm proud to be a member, offers valid proof that Jesus did indeed laugh. "We know that Jesus loved children, who laugh frequently and spontaneously." Samra rightly suggests that he also laughed "at the bumblings of his all-too-human disciples, who were missing the point and messing things up."

I wonder if the blast of sound we call laughter today might not have been what the psalmist had in mind when he wrote, "Shout joyfully to the LORD, all the earth" (Ps. 98:4). After all, they had other words for singing. And if two million Israelites stood around shouting "Hooray for God!" at the top of their lungs, somebody had to start laughing sooner or later.

—LIZ CURTIS HIGGS
Only Angels Can Wing It,
the Rest of Us Have to Practice

Putting More Laugh into Your Life

For you shall go out with joy,
And be led out with peace;
The mountains and the hills
Shall break forth into singing before you,
And all the trees of the field shall clap their hands.

—ISAIAH 55:12

I read somewhere that one way you can put more laughs into your life is to do something just plain outrageous. How long has it been since you have done something really GOOFY? Intentionally, I mean. Like jogging in triangles? Or driving in circles in a parking lot just for fun? Or going to the market wearing your wig inside out? I had gone quite awhile without enjoying some goofy fun, so Marilyn (my partner in crazy fun) and I decided to do something about it. We knew of a pastor who had been having some tremendous family problems and who was feeling down and depressed. He had said to me, "What I REALLY need is a visitation from the angels!"

Well, that was all we needed. The next day Marilyn and I went by our church, where we slipped into the baptismal room unnoticed and "borrowed" two long, full-flowing, baptismal robes. We drove over to our friend's home and stopped to don the robes about a block from his house. A mailman walking by nearly dropped his pouch when he saw two women get out of a Volvo and toss on these white robes with heavy weights in the bottom that sort of clinked as we walked.

When my husband, Bill, heard about our fun, he thought it was sacrilegious and unspiritual. His main concern was "Did you get the robes returned to the church?" But our pastor friend thought it was great. He got up in church and told everyone about these two women who came to give him a "visitation from the angels."

—BARBARA JOHNSON
So, Stick a Geranium in
Your Hat and Be Happy!

Releasing the Laughter

This is the day the LORD has made;
We will rejoice and be glad in it.

—PSALM 118:24

The late President John F. Kennedy believed in the value of laughter as a tension reliever. In the middle of the Cuban missile crisis, he was introduced to Bob Basso, who now runs a company called Laughter Therapy. Basso was then a navy lieutenant. As the president was preparing to meet with a group of advisors, he turned to Basso and said, "Lieutenant Basso, tell me a joke." Though Basso considered it an unusual time for joke telling, he did as the president requested. Kennedy apparently liked the joke and said he planned to use it to open the meeting. He later told Basso that humor was his greatest source of relieving tension; he said he doubted his ability to keep a balanced perspective without it.

What I am advocating here is not a mindless giggling through the serious events that touch our lives. Whether it is on a global, national, or personal level, I am suggesting that humor is often overlooked as an invaluable tension reliever. I believe we all have a tremendous potential to laugh, to see the humor in ourselves and in our experiences. I use the word *potential* because many of us have yet to realize our potential for humor. We frequently hear statements like, "Oh yes, he has a great sense of humor" or "She is so funny—I love to be around her" as if these favored few were unique and set apart by their capacity to create or appreciate humor. I believe we all have the capacity for fun and laughter. We do not all have the same abilities in creating humor—we are not all stand-up comics, but we can all laugh. Many of us, however, need to be released from the bondage of our circumstances and ourselves so that the inherent capacity to laugh, which lives in us all, can bubble to the surface and carry us through those times that are tension producing and spirit breaking.

—MARILYN MEBERG
Choosing the Amusing

Celebrating Enthusiasm

God willed to make known what are the riches of the glory of this mystery . . . which is Christ in you, the hope of glory.

—COLOSSIANS 1:27

For now we see in a mirror, dimly, but then face to face. Now I know in part, but then I shall know just as I also am known.

—1 CORINTHIANS 13:12

You know why I think it's such fun to learn something new? Because with every tidbit of information I get under my belt, it opens yet another door to a different adventure. It's never-ending! It introduces me to a multitude of fresh ideas and different ways of viewing circumstances and life as a whole. It makes me ask even more questions. It makes me enthusiastic about what's going to happen next on this journey called life. You see, real ongoing, lifelong education doesn't answer questions—it provokes them. It causes us to see that the fun and excitement of learning doesn't lie in having all the answers. It lies in the tension and the stretching of our minds between all the contradictory answers. It makes us think for ourselves. It frees us. It helps us grow up! That's where the fun comes in, where those surges of enthusiasm lie. That's where meaningful education takes place.

Even Scripture doesn't tell us every single thing we'd like to know. While it serves as a standard for living and a chart for life's course, much of it remains a secret. God designed it that way and that's okay. In fact, recently I heard my brother Chuck say during one of his Insight for Living broadcasts, "I find myself very comfortable when I come to Scripture that doesn't answer everything." I do too. That keeps us dependent upon God and having to live by faith. Fun, isn't it? And the fun's never going to stop!

—LUCI SWINDOLL
You Bring the Confetti,
God Brings the Joy

Celebrating Imagination

Now to him who is able to do immeasurably more than all we ask or imagine, according to his power that is at work within us, to him be glory . . . for ever and ever!

—EPHESIANS 3:20 NIV

*I*magination is a strange and many-splendored thing. It is the "stuff of which dreams are made." And where would we be without it? Thomas Edison, Wolfgang Amadeus Mozart, Orville and Wilbur Wright, William Shakespeare, Rembrandt and Picasso—the power of their imaginations changed our world.

Walt Disney—now there's a giant imagination for you. Think of the joy and fun it would have been to watch him work, to spend a whole day with him as ideas and concepts rolled out of his head. He once said that Disneyland really began when his two daughters were very young. They called Saturdays "Daddy's Day" and Walt Disney would take them to the park to ride the merry-go-round and play. While sitting alone on a bench eating peanuts and watching his children ride the painted horses on the carousel, he began to envision a kind of family park where parents and children could go to have fun together. His dream ultimately became the wonderful realities of Disneyland in Anaheim, California, and later Disneyworld in Orlando, Florida, two of the most magnificent and enormous amusement parks in the world. Because Disneyland had no precedent, there were no simple or tried-and-true solutions in its design or construction. Every single thing was unique. Isn't that fabulous? It *all* began in Walt Disney's head.

Webster defines *imagination* as:

> The action of forming mental images or concepts of what is not actually present to the senses; the faculty of producing ideal creations consistent with reality.

I call it "inventing the uninventable." Have you ever stopped to consider that every time you listen to music, turn on your television, read a book, go to a movie or a play or watch a comedian perform, every time you view a painting or a sculpture, it is the product of someone's imagination? Every invention and creation began with a "mental image or concept" of what was not actually present to the senses . . .

If you are blessed with a creative imagination, use it. Celebrate it! Keep it alive and well-oiled by constantly dreaming of inventions from which others will benefit. You don't have to build a Disneyland, but you can produce creative accomplishments in your own realm. Be imaginative and creative in your planning, during vacations, on your days off, at mealtimes, at parties, in your dress, in your décor. Make your own gift-wraps and greeting cards. Invent new recipes. Don't be afraid to let your mind try new ideas. Constantly look for the hidden possibilities in the obvious.

—LUCI SWINDOLL
You Bring the Confetti,
God Brings the Joy

Celebrating Who We Are

Our bodies have many parts, but the many parts make up only one body when they are all put together. So it is with the "body" of Christ.

—1 CORINTHIANS 12:12 NIV

I think it's time we celebrated who we are as women, in general, and as women of God, in particular. We can celebrate both our similarities and our differences. We may not look alike, we may have different gifts and abilities, but we are connected in the Spirit. We share a common bond in Christ but speak with different voices and from different life experiences. Each of us has something unique to offer.

That's good. I don't want to be like everybody else. Some women like it simple, and others like it soft; some prefer life with a little spice, and some can take it with salsa. I happen to like mine with a little soul. *Vive la difference!*

The way we approach life varies according to our tastes, our culture, our environment—all the forces that shape us and make us who we are. But most of all, it depends on how we relate to

God. When we appreciate whose we are, we are able to respond favorably to others who are also in the Spirit, even if their approaches are not the same as our own. We can celebrate who we are.

—SUZAN JOHNSON COOK
Too Blessed to Be Stressed

Celebrating Femininity

Charm is deceitful and beauty is passing,
But a woman who fears the LORD, she shall be praised.

—PROVERBS 31:30

I love being a woman! I celebrate my femininity. I appreciate lovely times, soft surroundings, poetic verbiage, romantic trysts, finger-long lace, tea parties, floral bouquets, and shopping until my Rockports rot. I'm thrilled to have Eve qualities that set me apart from the Adams of this world. I prefer being the main nurturer and cheerleader of humankind. I take delight in the distinctive differences, in our feminine nuances that add to a woman's mystery and appeal. I'm pleased I'm considered huggable, reliable, and pleasurable.

I'm proud that history proves us gals to be competent, courageous, innovative, and invaluable. I stand taller to be named with those who have gone before us, from Old Testament Deborah and Ruth to New Testament Lydia, from Florence Nightingale to Corrie ten Boom. We have rocked cradles, ruled nations, and succeeded as entrepreneurs. We have successfully encouraged men and children on to their personal victories. Yes, yes, I do love being a woman.

—PATSY CLAIRMONT
I Love Being a Woman

Recalling the Source of Our Cheer

The LORD is gracious and full of compassion,
Slow to anger and great in mercy.
The LORD is good to all,
And His tender mercies are over all His works.

—PSALM 145:8–9

I am convinced that one of life's most easily accessible sources of cheer is to remember some of the off-the-wall, crazy things that happen to us . . . it doesn't have to be a Big Moment, just something zany and fun. Sometimes those memories are bittersweet as we recall an out-of-the-ordinary moment with a loved one who is now gone. But those times nevertheless provide cheer because that was the emotion felt when the experience occurred. That original cheerful feeling will always remain attached to that memory.

Now if all of this sounds like preparation for successful retirement at the "home," where you sit on the porch rocking, picking your teeth, smiling vacantly as you accept your afternoon tapioca, and reminiscing, I want to say that just isn't the case. Pleasant memories can give us an immediate cheer-producing mind switch. We don't have to wait until we're seventy to do it! Those memories can be as recent as this morning or as distant as thirty years ago. All that matters is that the quirky memory cheers you.

Incidentally, the whole "remembering" thing is a biblical concept. God was continually urging His people to remember what He had done for them as a means of encouragement. He wanted them to remember "that God was their Rock, that God Most High was their Redeemer" (Ps. 78:35). I love the image in Malachi 3:16, "A scroll of remembrance was written in his presence concerning those who feared the Lord and honored his name."

Can't you just picture that scroll of remembrance? I see it as being miles long with tight, black-ink writing all over it. Maybe a huge magnifying glass is nearby for reading the fine-print remembrances. The very thought gives me an unexpected perk!

For us believers, remembering starts out by recalling God is the source of our cheer. From that foundational position, we can move into the human realm and remember those experiences that were cheer producing.

—MARILYN MEBERG
I'd Rather Be Laughing

Sensational Encouragement

Words of Comfort,
Peace, and Hope

All the Way My Savior Leads Me

For the Lamb . . . will shepherd them and lead them to living foun-tains of waters.

—REVELATION 7:17

All the way my Savior leads me
What have I to ask beside?
Can I doubt His tender mercy,
Who through life has been my Guide?
Heav'nly peace, divinest comfort,
Here by faith in Him to dwell!
For I know, whate'er befall me,
Jesus doeth all things well;
For I know, whate'er befall me,
Jesus doeth all things well.

All the way my Savior leads me
Cheers each winding path I tread,
Gives me grace for every trial,

Feeds me with the living Bread.
Though my weary steps may falter
And my soul athirst may be,
Gushing from the Rock before me,
Lo! A spring of joy I see;
Gushing from the Rock before me,
Lo! A spring of joy I see.

All the way my Savior leads me
O the fullness of His love!
Perfect rest to me is promised
In my Father's house above.
When my spirit, clothed immortal,
Wings its flight to realms of day
This my song through endless ages:
Jesus led me all the way;
This my song through endless ages:
Jesus led me all the way.

—FANNY J. CROSBY

Clinging to Our Hope

Have you not known?

Have you not heard?

The everlasting God, the LORD,

The Creator of the ends of the earth,

Neither faints nor is weary.

His understanding is unsearchable.

He gives power to the weak,

And to those who have no might He increases strength.

Even the youths shall faint and be weary,

And the young men shall utterly fall,

But those who wait on the LORD

Shall renew their strength;

They shall mount up with wings like eagles,

They shall run and not be weary,

They shall walk and not faint.

—ISAIAH 40:28–31

When you find yourself sliding toward the end of the rope, tie a KNOT and hang on. And do you know what that knot at the end of the rope is? IT IS HOPE, and our hope is JESUS!

If we say a situation is hopeless, we are slamming the door in the face of God. Instead, we have to be like the little boy who stood so long at the top of the escalator, watching intently, until someone asked him what he was doing. He patiently replied, "I stuck my chewing gum on that black hand rail, and I'm waiting for it to come back!"

Like the little boy, we must believe that our happiness WILL come back. The misery WILL end, and our joy will return to us.

—BARBARA JOHNSON
I'm So Glad You Told Me
What I Didn't Wanna Hear

The Heart's True Home

Let not your heart be troubled; you believe in God, believe also in Me. In My Father's house are many mansions; if it were not so, I would have told you. I go to prepare a place for you. And if I go and prepare a place for you, I will come again and receive you to Myself; that where I am, there you may be also.

—JOHN 14:1–3

These words of Jesus are among the most comforting in all Scripture. Jesus looks directly into our hearts and sees that we are troubled, worried, and anxious. "You believe in God," he says, "believe also in me." Subtly, Jesus tells us not to believe in the anxiety we harbor in our hearts; he directs our focus away from our hearts' trouble to our hearts' home. Notice that Jesus doesn't tell us to get a grip on ourselves, to stop worrying, and to get control of whatever is troubling us. He doesn't even tell us to think positively or pray harder. Jesus isn't into spiritual self-help. Neither does He dismiss our troubles as silly or even sinful. Instead, Jesus welcomes our troubled and anxious hearts into the

Father's house, a house with many rooms. And one of those rooms has our name on it. We are to come home to live with Jesus.

The best remedy for anxiety is living with Jesus every day. Jesus opens wide the door of his Father's house to welcome us home, troubled hearts and all. For the grace of God is greater than all of our worst worries; the love of God bears all of our worst imaginings; the mercy of God is deeper than our worst fears. Jesus makes his home with us, and any house, no matter how humble or how grand, is home when we open our hearts to the presence of Christ.

—HARRIET CROSBY
A Place Called Home

That Blessed Hope

The LORD is good to those who wait for Him,
To the soul who seeks Him.
It is good that one should hope and wait quietly
For the salvation of the LORD.

—LAMENTATIONS 3:25–26

$\mathcal{W}$hen biblical writers used the word "hope," they usually did not mean "wishing something were so." The biblical concept was more of a settled anticipation, a favorable and constant expectation. The Greek verb form for *hope* used in the New Testament frequently is related to the concept of trust. For example, in Titus 2:13, Christ is called "that blessed hope"(KJV) . . .

Even when we've landed with our faces in the dust, even when we are caught in a wringer, we can always have hope. And even when hope is lost, it can be regained; we can refocus our perspective. As we wait on the Lord, our strength will be renewed and so will our joy. In the Scriptures, hope and joy always go together. I like to say hope and joy are sisters.

Hope is God's holding power that gives a consistent flow of joy deep beneath the waves of trouble in the winds of sorrow. Hope invades the mind and heart with joy and gives us the deep confidence that we are God's forgiven children and that He will never let us go.

—BARBARA JOHNSON
Pack Up Your Gloomees in a
Great Big Box Then Sit on
the Lid and Laugh

Jesus Is Enough

Then you shall call, and the LORD will answer;
You shall cry, and He will say,
"Here I am."

—ISAIAH 58:9

*L*iving our lives with certain things unresolved is what faith is all about. I believe that many things happen that we simply can't explain. When we look back after many years, we still have little understanding of what went on. But we have the knowledge and assurance that Jesus was there with us through every moment, walking by our side, guiding our footsteps. We never needed to fear the questions, because Jesus was answer enough.

Some of the greatest words Paul ever wrote start with questions: Can anything separate us from the love Christ has for us? Can troubles or problems or sufferings? If we have no food or clothes, if we are in danger, or even if death comes, can any of these things separate us from Christ's love?

Paul's answer is that nothing—*absolutely nothing*—in this

entire world can separate us from the love of God that is in Christ Jesus our Lord . . .

Here is where we must start. Even in the darkest night, the most blinding pain, the most maddening frustration—when nothing makes sense anymore—we keep going because He alone is worth it all.

For years I drank deeply of the false belief that if I just had enough faith everything would go my way. I thought I had God in a box: I do this for God and He does that for me. But it's not true, and so many lives are caught and wrecked in the wake of this teaching.

"What did I do wrong?" we cry. Heaven cries back, "Everything, but I love you anyway. Always have, always will." . . .

Holding on is hard—it can seem impossible—but it is worth it because Jesus is worth it. No matter what happens, Jesus is enough.

—SHEILA WALSH
Life Is Tough But God Is Faithful

Dropping the Tangles of Life

The LORD also will be a refuge for the oppressed,
A refuge in times of trouble.
And those who know Your name will put their trust in You;
For You, LORD, have not forsaken those who seek You.

—PSALM 9:9–10

*H*ope is the essential ingredient to make it through life. It is the anchor of the soul. The Lord is good to those who hope in Him. If your hope is gone, it can be rekindled. You can regain hope—you can refocus your view and wait on the Lord to renew your strength . . .

Think of your life, with all the mistakes, sins, and woes of the past, like the tangles in a ball of yarn. It's such a mess that you could never begin to straighten it out. It is such a *comfort* to drop the tangles of life into God's hands, and then LEAVE THEM THERE. If there is one message I want to share with you, it is to place your child, your spouse, your friends, whomever it might be, in God's hands and *release* the load to Him. God alone can untangle the threads of our lives. WHAT A JOY AND COMFORT IT CAN BE TO DROP ALL THE TANGLES OF LIFE INTO GOD'S HANDS AND THEN SIMPLY LEAVE THEM THERE! That's what hope is all about.

—BARBARA JOHNSON
So, Stick a Geranium in Your Hat and Be Happy!

Being Anxious for Nothing

The LORD will perfect that which concerns me;
Your mercy, O LORD, endures forever;
Do not forsake the works of Your hands.

—PSALM 138:8

A few years ago in the month of January, I was praying for God to give me a scripture that would sustain me in the coming months. When I got off my knees, I turned on Christian television, and there was a man saying, "Some of you want to know a scripture that will help you during this year. Turn in your Bibles to Philippians 4, and read with me."

I hurriedly opened my Bible to Philippians and started reading along with the preacher. When we got to the sixth verse, I knew that God wanted me to read, chew on, swallow, and digest these words for that year: "Be anxious for nothing. But in all things with prayer and supplication, with thanksgiving, let your petition be made known to God, and the God of peace which surpasses understanding will guard your heart and your mind, through Christ Jesus."

Little did I know that the year was going to start and finish with me having to remind myself of that scripture more times than I wanted be reminded! That was a tough year for me. If I had not meditated constantly on that specific scripture, I don't think I would have made it. But I did what the verse said: I took petition after petition straight to God, and with a thankful heart that didn't leave room for anxiety, I left all my requests with Him. And you know what? He took care of them. Not always in the exact way I wanted, but in the exact way I needed.

When God promises peace, Sister, He means peace! Take Him at His *Word*!

—THELMA WELLS
*Girl, Have I Got Good
News for You*

God Alone Can Hold Us

When you pass through the waters, I will be with you;
And through the rivers, they shall not overflow you.
When you walk through the fire, you shall not be burned,
Nor shall the flame scorch you.

—ISAIAH 43:2

My soul waits for the Lord
More than those who watch for the morning—
Yes, more than those who watch for the morning.

—PSALM 130:6

*P*erfect peace is translated from the Hebrew *shalom shalom*, which signifies *fulfillment, abundance, well-being, security.* The phrase *whose mind is stayed on You* comes from two Hebrew words: the first meaning "will, imagination"; the second, "dependent, supported, firm." When our wills and imaginations are dependent on God, when we choose to turn our thoughts to Him, we can find the simple truth that God is enough. We find out, as Isaiah wrote, that "in the LORD is everlasting strength." And in His strength we discover fulfillment and security.

Our faith in God is not enough to bring about miracles. God takes home some faithful servants before we are ready to say good-bye. And He allows people with no faith at all to be healed. All we can do in the time of grief is to set our minds on Him, to believe God is enough even if the miracles don't come, for He alone can hold us through the night.

—SHEILA WALSH
Life Is Tough But God Is Faithful

His Promised Peace and Protection

I will both lie down in peace, and sleep;
For You alone, O Lord, make me dwell in safety.

—PSALM 4:8

My daughter Vikki was independent, adventurous, and courageous as a twenty-something young lady, and she had always wanted to see the world. She set out on an eighteen-country tour, and the first six months of her voyage from Dallas to Europe, Asia, and India went well. The next stop was to be Egypt, but God intervened.

She called me from an airport in India and said, "I'm not going on to Egypt as I'd planned. Something's telling me I need to leave and go to Germany. I'll call you in a few days when I get there."

Little did she know that the day after her departure, the day she was scheduled to be in Egypt, war broke out. Operation Desert Storm had begun. Had she gone to Egypt or remained in that area of the world, the possibility of her getting trapped there by the military is frightening to think about. Many Americans were caught there and were not permitted to leave for a number of days . . .

In every situation, whether ordinary or life threatening, God assures us that He keeps His eye on us and knows the number of hairs on our heads. Absolutely everything that can happen to us—good, bad, or indifferent—God knows and cares about. God is concerned about us all the time, in every area of our lives, even if nobody else is. He promises that we are never away from His presence.

Does that mean nothing bad will ever happen to us? No. But is does mean that we can have inner peace in this dangerous world. Jesus declared, "I have told you these things, so that in me you may have peace. In this world you will have trouble. But take heart! I have overcome the world" (John 16:33 NIV).

God has promised to watch over His dominion children. Every trial, tribulation, question mark, perplexity, decision, burden, disappointment, heartache, calamity, tragedy, turmoil, loss, danger, exclusion, accusation, threat, or act of the devil is within the scope of God's knowledge and care. He is sovereign, and He knows the outcome of whatever befalls us. He has already worked it out. His ministering angels protect us. His precious blood covers us. His grace and mercy go before us.

—THELMA WELLS
What's Going On, Lord?

Riding to the Shores of Truth and Safety

Peace I leave with you, My peace I give to you; not as the world gives do I give to you. Let not your heart be troubled, neither let it be afraid.

—JOHN 14:27

Mercy, peace, and love be multiplied to you.

—JUDE 2

As an emotional and fragile woman who has faced many valleys and "dark nights of the soul," I can speak to you sincerely and confidently about the unwavering love and mercy of Jesus Christ.

I am single yet comforted by the ultimate bridegroom.

I was orphaned by having two young parents taken from this earth, but have been adopted by the Father of the fatherless.

I have struggled with weight issues and yet continue to hear Him affirm my femininity with words of beauty as He escorts me through this life.

I can worry about finances, and He'll reassure me that His eye is on the sparrow.

When I'm prideful He humbly embraces me.

My self-esteem hits all-time lows, and He'll whisper my worth through the cross.

I've forsaken Him. He's forgiven me.

I'll get hit with waves of anxiety and doubt, and He'll allow me to ride above them to shores of truth and safety as I learn to put my trust in Him.

—KATHY TROCCOLI
Different Roads

Finding Peace in Stillness

You will keep him in perfect peace,
Whose mind is stayed on You,
Because he trusts in You.

—ISAIAH 26:3

Meditate within your heart . . . and be still.
Offer the sacrifices of righteousness,
And put your trust in the LORD.

—PSALM 4:4–5

*I*t's a fact of life. Because I'm paralyzed from the shoulders down, a large part of me never moves. I don't run; I sit. I don't race; I wait. My body is in constant repose. My upright, sitting-straight position is never changing. Even when my wheels are tracking miles beneath me, I stay put. I can be scurrying through a jam-packed schedule, doing this and that, but a big part of me—due to my paralysis—is always quiet. Always tranquil . . .

But it hasn't always been that way. My "natural" stillness used to drive me crazy. After my diving injury, I laid still for three months waiting to be moved from the intensive care unit into a regular hospital room. After more months of lying still, I was finally moved to a rehabilitation center. While in rehab, I stayed put in my wheelchair for hours outside of physical therapy, waiting my turn to go in. And in the evenings, my manufactured stillness would madden me as I sat by the door waiting for friends or family to come for a visit . . .

But time, prayer, and study in God's Word have a way of changing many things. And somewhere in the ensuing years, I discovered that the weakness of those claustrophobic hours was the key to God's peace and power. My enforced stillness was God's way of conforming the inside to what had happened on the outside . . .

Now, many years later, my bed is an altar of praise. It's the one spot on this harried planet where I always meet God in relaxed stillness. In fact, as soon as I wheel into my bedroom and see the bed covers pulled back my mind immediately responds, *It's time to be still and know more about God. It's time to pray.*

It can be the same for you. When you find yourself in forced stillness—waiting in line, sitting by a hospital bed, or stuck in traffic—instead of fidgeting and fuming, use such moments to practice stillness before God.

It's a crazy world and life speeds by at a blur, yet God is right in the middle of the craziness. And anywhere, at anytime, we may turn to Him, hear His voice, feel His hand and catch the fragrance of heaven.

You can be still and know that He is God. And you don't have to break your neck to find out.

—JONI EARECKSON TADA

Holiness in Hidden Places

An Endless Calm

Oh, the depth of the riches both of the wisdom and knowledge of God! How unsearchable are His judgments and His ways past finding out!

—ROMANS 11:33

Though there's a majestic and powerful beauty on the surface of the ocean, there's even more beauty when you dive beneath the waves. Even as a kid with a face mask on, I'd dive and discover a world of endless calm—luxuriant seaweed swaying gracefully, colorful shells, small fish darting here and there . . . a world that's quiet and deep.

When you dive beneath the surface things of God, you also discover an endless calm—a world of divine life that is quiet and deep. There, in the depths, God will reveal a quiet and gentle kind of interior beauty.

The Lord is so generous! Even when we choose to live only on the surface of things, where we're often tossed this way and that. God still reveals Himself through thrilling displays of His power.

But there's much more to God than what you see—what we all see of Him—on the surface.

When we dive deeper into God's heart, all the turmoil of our daily lives—the problems that crash around us like huge waves—seem somehow . . . distant. The roar is like a far-away echo of thunderous waves "falling sweet as a far off psalm" . . . Frances Havergal [writes],

> There are strange, soul depths,
> Restless and vast, unfathomed as the sea.
> An infinite craving for some infinite stilling.
> And, lo, His perfect love is perfect filling.
> Lord Jesus Christ, my lord and my God,
> Thou, thou are enough for me.

—JONI EARECKSON TADA
Holiness in Hidden Places

He Is the Prince of Peace

Be anxious for nothing, but in everything by prayer and supplication, with thanksgiving, let your requests be made known to God; and the peace of God, which surpasses all understanding, will guard your hearts and minds through Christ Jesus.

—PHILIPPIANS 4:6–7

*E*xperience Peace Daily" was my heart-framed piece of encouragement for 1995, on display near the bathroom mirror where I was sure to read it often. I've found I can experience such peace anytime, anywhere, by doing two things: praying and breathing.

"Praying, sure, but breathing?" you say. "I do that all the time!"

That's what I thought, too, until Lois taught me how to do peace-filled breathing.

Choose a straight-back chair, set your feet on the floor, and place your hands in your lap or by your side. Silence helps but isn't necessary, because I've done this in crowded airports or at the dinner table when the conversation sounded more like war than peace.

Breathe deeply and evenly, through your nose, all the way down to the base of your spine. When you can hold no more, pause for a beat or two and begin to let the air out v-e-r-y slowly through your mouth. Just open your lips and let it flow out; no need to hiss and blow like the wind, just nice and easy. I love to meditate on this verse while I'm at it: "Peace I leave with you, My peace I give to you" (John 14:27), or another favorite, "And let the peace of God rule in your hearts" (Col. 3:15) . . .

Just as we are sometimes encouraged to tighten all our muscles, then relax them one by one as a method of physical stress reduction, I have found the same concept works with thoughts of peacefulness.

First, think of all the words that are the *opposite* of peace: shouting, turmoil, chaos, conflict, hostility, violence, pain, suffering, war, death. *Ugh.*

Then, concentrate on peaceful words: quiet, calm, contentment, serenity, tranquillity, harmony, healing, relief, life, love, and Jesus. *Ahhh.*

He is the Prince, the Ruler, the Source of Peace. Real peace can only come from him. Anything else, even breathing, is temporary and of the flesh. It's just an aid to get you where you want to be: in his peaceful presence.

—LIZ CURTIS HIGGS
Mirror, Mirror on the Wall,
Have I Got News for You!

Finding Peace through Acceptance

. . . I know whom I have believed and am persuaded that He is able to keep what I have committed to Him until that Day.

—2 TIMOTHY 1:12

The way I respond to the "givens" in my daily experience determines my growth in holiness. When we pray, "Give us this day our daily bread," God answers that prayer, measuring out just what we need for spiritual as well as physical growth. He knows that spiritual stamina cannot develop without conflict. We must take with both hands the thing given, submissively, humbly, sometimes courageously, or even, as one friend put it, "defiantly"—saying to ourselves, *This is part of the story,* the story of the love of God for me and of my love for Him.

This is acceptance in the truest sense. This is where real peace is found—that strange, inexplicable peace Jesus promised.

—ELISABETH ELLIOT
The Path of Loneliness

God's Healing Presence

My brethren, count it all joy when you fall into various trials, knowing
that the testing of your faith produces patience. But let patience have its
perfect work, that you may be perfect and complete, lacking nothing.

—JAMES 1:2–4

We talk about grief and hardship as time spent in "the valley." But later, looking back from the hilltop, we see that it was there, in that valley, that we became better persons, selfless servants, stronger Christians. As my daughter-in-love, Shannon, says, we grow when we're down in the valley, because that's where the fertilizer is!

We have two choices when we're faced with suffering and tragedy. One is to withdraw from life, become bitter, and die inwardly. The other is to reach out to God in whatever way we can and allow Him to use our sorrow for good. When we welcome God's healing presence into our broken lives, we're soon amazed to find His spirit propelling us to reach out to others who are hurting, offering encouragement wherever we find sorrow. Before too long, we realize that true happiness comes by helping others and knowing we are appreciated, even if all we've done is make ourselves available to care and to listen.

In the depths of our misery, we might not have thought ourselves capable of such a turnaround. We might never have pictured ourselves doing the thoughtful deeds we find ourselves doing. And yet there we are, turning misery into ministry.

By sacrificing our energy on behalf of others, we discover there is a priceless reward for those who devote their lives to God's service. Every word spoken to the sorrowful, every act committed to relieve the oppressed, every kindness shown to the brokenhearted will result in blessings, not only to the sufferer, but also to the giver. I love to call this phenomenon "boomerang blessings."

We are refreshed by encouragement when we know others have benefited from our efforts. We are blessed with a warm satisfaction when we allow ourselves to be used in God's service. As He uses us, He transforms our lives in the same way He changes a piece of coal into a diamond. Our tears crystallize into sparkling jewels of blessing that sparkle in the night of despair "like the stars of the morning," shining out in the darkness with the light of God's embracing, sustaining love.

—BARBARA JOHNSON
God's Most Precious Jewels
Are Crystallized Tears

God Knows What You Need

But you, when you pray, go into your room, and when you have shut
your door, pray to your Father who is in the secret place; and your
Father who sees in secret will reward you openly. And when you pray,
do not use vain repetitions as the heathen do. For they think they will
be heard for their many words. Therefore do not be like them. For
your Father knows the things you have need of before you ask Him.

—MATTHEW 6:6–8

The disciples were so right when they asked Jesus to teach them to pray. We all prayed [for my mother-in-law, Eleanor], "God, heal her." Eleanor went to all sorts of healing meetings, even one in the final month at her own church. I think it was one of those strange paradoxes of the kingdom of God that our prayers were answered in ways we did not expect: the peace she found in the last moments of her life, the intimacy with her family, and the joy that she is now experiencing in finally being home. God healed her in ways much greater than she or I could ever have put into words.

Eleanor and I found joy with tear-stained faces. I began to see how caught up we are in the "now," in what we think will make us happy this minute. We run around like squirrels, gathering stuff, never stopping, wondering why we don't feel loved.

I've decided to change the way I pray. I used to pray with a whole long list of things I wanted God to do; now I pray for wisdom, and I pray to be more like Christ. My friend Marilyn Meberg once asked Orville Swindoll, Luci's big brother, "What is the most important thing you learned during your life on the mission field?" I love his reply: "I used to think the most important thing was to be right. Now I know it's to become like Jesus Christ."

Amen, Orville. What joy!

—SHEILA WALSH
Unexpected Grace

God Shines Through
the Broken Places

*Commit your way to the L*ORD,
Trust also in Him,
And He shall bring it to pass.
He shall bring forth your righteousness as the light,
And your justice as the noonday.
*Rest in the L*ORD, *and wait patiently for Him.*

—PSALM 37:5–7

*A*unt Mary, the matriarch of our family, was holding on through failing health to meet [my son, Christian,] the newest "little lamb." It would be a lovely Christmas. When we arrived at Mum's house, packages galore were under her tree . . .

Standing on the Scottish soil on which I was raised, I felt like Job. I felt as if I had come full circle. The grace and mercy that God had poured into my life suddenly overwhelmed me.

I remembered the tears I had shed as a child, not understanding why I had to be the only girl in my class with no dad. I remembered the awkward teenage years, hating my body as it started to develop, feeling embarrassed and unlovable because of my greasy hair and bad skin. I remembered the years of running at full speed for God, trying to impress Him with my manic devotion. I remembered the first few days in that psychiatric ward, feeling hopeless and sad and lost.

Now as I stood at the edge of the cold winter sea, I was wrapped in God's blanket of love. Just ahead of me, running like the wind chasing sea gulls, was my two-year-old bundle of grace and joy. Beside me was Barry, my wonderful, loving, funny, kind husband. Tucked into the pockets of my soul were two years of sharing my life with women all across the country and seeing with my own eyes the way that God shines through the broken places of our lives, bringing hope and life. It seemed so kind to be given this gift on my native soil. It made me want to get down on my knees and worship.

I knew then that the moment wouldn't be so sweet if I had known the future at any time along the way. For the agony of past moments of despair made this moment even more miraculous and joyful. The contrast was so great! The moment so glowing. Yes, God is faithful.

—SHEILA WALSH
Life Is Tough But God Is Faithful

Waiting for God's Plan

In You, O LORD, I put my trust;
Let me never be put to shame.
Deliver me in Your righteousness, and cause me to escape;
Incline Your ear to me, and save me . . .
For You are my hope, O Lord GOD;
You are my trust from my youth.

—PSALM 71:1–2, 5

God allows us to be in the wilderness—in fact, sometimes He is glad to put us in the wilderness—so that our faith will grow. We're so fickle. Often, we don't hang on to Him when everything is bright and prosperous . . .

Though He allows us to go through the wilderness, . . . He still grieves for the pain we feel. He sees our tears and He cares. I love the verse that says:

You have collected all my tears and preserved them in your bottle!
(Psalm 56:8*b* TLB)

How attentive, how intimate of God to be aware of my tears. Not one of them is casually discarded by Him.

How long will we cry? How long will we be in the wilderness before the sun breaks through, before the weight is lifted? Only God knows, but in His knowing, He will surely provide all the grace we need during the times we feel so weak, lonely, and confused.

If it were us, we might have had Jesus raised up on the first day, or maybe the second. God waited until the third day because He was accomplishing His perfect will. He had a plan. He has a plan for each and every one of us. We must wait for it.

—KATHY TROCCOLI
Falling in Love with Jesus

Your Shepherd's Arms

Yea, though I walk through the valley of the shadow of death,
I will fear no evil;
For You are with me;
Your rod and Your staff, they comfort me.

—PSALM 23:4

*P*aul knew about persecution and loneliness from both sides of the fence. For he (Saul) not only persecuted others for their faith, but he (Paul—new name) also suffered at the hands of others for his faith. Perhaps it was in lonely moments that he wrote, "For our citizenship is in heaven, from which also we eagerly wait for a Savior, the Lord Jesus Christ" (Phil. 3:20), and "We . . . prefer rather to be absent from the body and to be at home with the Lord" (2 Cor. 5:8).

At some point in his dramatic life, Paul realized we weren't going to be at home totally (even with ourselves) until we stepped on heaven's shore. Then the disturbing distance between us and others would disappear. Any disconnected feeling between us and the Lord would be over, and our inner and outer struggles with loneliness would be eternally resolved. Until then, we need to keep on keeping on. It's not easy to carry on when you're feeling alone, which is why it's important to expect to feel separation at times (from God, others, and ourselves) as part of our fallen condition. That way, the long-distance times can't sneak up on us and leave us distraught, but we can lean into our loneliness and learn.

Jesus promised never to leave us, and He is a promise keeper. Our times of loneliness don't testify to His absence in our lives, but rather the loneliness allows us to feel our human dilemma (of limitations) from which only He can rescue us. The Lord didn't say He would shelter us from the full range of human emotions, from joy to devastation and from sweet fellowship to acute loneliness. Our emotions don't alter God's constancy in our lives. Instead, negative emotions often prompt us to search out the positive principles of His unfailing presence.

One of the tender artistic portrayals of Christ as shepherd that stands out in my mind is entitled "Lost Lamb." The artist shows Christ as He leans over the side of a cliff and extends His shepherd's crook around a bewildered lamb on a ledge. You know He will then draw the lonely creature into the safety of His arms.

The next time you feel lost and lonely, remember there is One who longs for you to know you're not alone. The good Shepherd knows you by name and He will travel the long distance on your behalf. He will search the widest pasture, the steepest highlands, the deepest valley, and even the most desolate desert to help you find your way, so intense is His love for you.

—PATSY CLAIRMONT
Sportin' a 'Tude

Accepting the Imperfections

*These things I have spoken to you, that in Me you may have peace.
In the world you will have tribulation; but be of good cheer, I have
overcome the world.*

—JOHN 16:33

*He has made everything beautiful in its time. Also He has put eter-
nity in their hearts, except that no one can find out the work that
God does from beginning to end.*

—ECCLESIASTES 3:11–12

We were created for perfection. In fact, we were originally placed in a perfect environment. In Eden there were no linger-ing headaches, digestive challenges, or unsettling scandals. No house would be too large, too small, or too far from the beach. God would supply our desire for the perfect mate as He brought that perfect other to us. God's original design for each of us was to live in a state of perfection. We were created for that experi-ence, and we were created for that expectation.

So what happened? . . .

Let's repeat: Imperfection, trials, and sorrows all started with disobedience in the Garden. Eve fell for a Satan-devised lie, drew her buck-passing husband into it all, and lost paradise. But we can be of good cheer because Christ has overcome the deficits accrued to our account because of Eden.

Nothing in life is perfect because perfection was lost in Eden. But the flip side of this negative is fully understanding and accepting that life will never be perfect and neither will any experience or relationship. If we can accept that, we can quit looking for it, blaming others or ourselves because we can't find it, and even come to a place of peace about that loss. In fact, we might even cheer up a bit as we quit the search . . . the pressure to find perfection is over.

—MARILYN MEBERG
I'd Rather Be Laughing

Suffering Is Like Baking a Cake

Now thanks be to God who always leads us in triumph in Christ,
and through us diffuses the fragrance of His knowledge in every place.

—2 CORINTHIANS 2:14

I like to compare suffering to making a cake. No one sits down, gets out a box of baking powder, eats a big spoonful, and says, "Hmmm, that's good!" And you don't do that with a spoonful of shortening or raw eggs or flour, either. The tribulation and suffering in our lives can be compared with swallowing a spoonful of baking powder or shortening. By themselves these things are distasteful and they turn your stomach. But God takes all of these ingredients, stirs them up, and puts them in His own special oven. He knows just how long to let the cake bake; sometimes it stays in God's oven for YEARS. We get impatient and want to open the oven, thinking, *Surely the cake must be done by now.* But not yet, no not yet. What really matters is that the cake is BAKING and the marvelous aroma is filling the house.

I find that people who trust God with their suffering have an invisible something, like the invisible aroma of a freshly baked cake, that draws people to them. As Paul put it, "all things [all the ingredients of pain and suffering] work together for good to them that love God" (Rom. 8:28 KJV).

When we believe that nothing comes to us except through our heavenly Father, then suffering begins to make a little sense to us—not much, I admit, but a little bit, and that's all God needs to work in our lives, just a mustard seed of faith. Then we can see that God is using our pain to work something in us that is redemptive. Every trial or broken relationship goes into God's oven and eventually we begin to "smell" like cake or fresh bread. Even our suffering counts for something!

—BARBARA JOHNSON
Pack Up Your Gloomees in a
Great Big Box Then Sit on the
Lid and Laugh

Sensational Faith

Wisdom and Guidance
for the Journey

Close to Thee

Thou my everlasting Portion,
More than friend or life to me,
All along my pilgrim journey,
Savior, let me walk with Thee.

Close to Thee, close to Thee,
Close to Thee, close to Thee,
All along my pilgrim journey,
Savior, let me walk with Thee.

Not for ease or worldly pleasure,
Nor for fame my prayer shall be;
Gladly will I toil and suffer,
Only let me walk with Thee.

Close to Thee, close to Thee,
Close to Thee, close to Thee,
Gladly will I toil and suffer,
Only let me walk with Thee.

Lead me through the vale of shadows,
Bear me over life's fitful sea;
Then the gate of life eternal
May I enter, Lord, with Thee.

Close to Thee, close to Thee,
Close to Thee, close to Thee,
Then the gate of life eternal
May I enter, Lord, with Thee.

—FANNY J. CROSBY

You Grow as You Go

Now faith is the substance of things hoped for,
the evidence of things not seen.

—HEBREWS 11:1

For we walk by faith, not by sight.

—2 CORINTHIANS 5:7

My pastor gave an illustration that is the perfect picture of faith: You arrive at the airport, baggage in both hands. You approach the closed door and wonder how you can get the door open with your arms so full of baggage. How, indeed? All that is necessary is to take one more step. The doors open automatically.

Or suppose you are walking on a very dark night using only a small flashlight. The light makes a circle immediately in front of you. Only as you take the next step does the light move out in front.

Do you see? Take just one more step and you will be given the faith and the power to add another step, and another. You grow as you go.

—SUZANNE DALE EZELL
*Living Simply in God's
Abundance*

Stretching Your Measure of Faith

But without faith it is impossible to please Him, for he who comes to God must believe that He is, and that He is a rewarder of those who diligently seek Him.

—HEBREWS 11:6

I used to think it was wrong to ascribe different levels to people's faith, as though some were better than others. But Jesus did. He said of one individual in Matthew 14:31, "You of little faith . . ." and then a chapter later He said, "Woman, you have great faith!" Yet it has nothing to do with one person being better than the next. The apostle Paul wrote in Romans 12:3, "Do not think of yourself more highly than you ought, but rather think of yourself with sober judgment, *in accordance with the measure of faith God has given you*" (emphasis added).

Faith, you see, is a gift from God. And, really, it's not the size of that faith that matters. Jesus says your faith could be the size of a mustard seed and great things could still happen.

How do we take this measure of faith God gives us and make

it . . . extraordinary? It's all a matter of focus. "Faith is being sure of what we hope for and certain of what we do not see" (Heb. 11:1). So faith is being sure of something you hope for—that is, sure about unfulfilled things in the future. And it's being certain of something you can't see—that is, being keenly aware of the unseen divine realities all around you.

Faith makes that which is unseen, real. And that which is seen, much less important.

Great faith means focusing on the King and His kingdom priorities . . . We are in the minor leagues down here on earth, training for the major leagues in heaven. Each of us has been given a measure of faith and, with it, we train ourselves in godliness. We work with the equipment God has given us, stretching our faith muscles. And what happens when He calls you up to the plate and pitches you a fastball? You *connect*. You hit a line drive, if not a home run. You make it your ambition to be pleasing to Him.

—JONI EARECKSON TADA
Ordinary People,
Extraordinary Faith

Walking by Faith

I have set the LORD always before me;

Because He is at my right hand I shall not be moved.

Therefore my heart is glad, and my glory rejoices;

My flesh also will rest in hope . . .

You will show me the path of life;

In Your presence is fullness of joy;

At Your right hand are pleasures forevermore.

—PSALM 16:8–9, 11

*L*orne Sanny, a past president of The Navigators, shared a story of how many years earlier he had been taking his young son on a walk. The little boy was running ahead of him, looking at rocks and bugs, when suddenly a large dog appeared on the trail. Lorne's son came running back to him, wide-eyed, and immediately grabbed his father's hand. Then he turned back around and said bravely, "Hi, big dog!"

This is a good illustration of walking by faith. As a new creation in Christ, I can take hold of His hand and walk confidently through the world. It doesn't mean that I will not have to face lions, fiery furnaces, or armies, but I do not have to fear them. My faith is in the living God, and my life is hidden with Christ. In reality, the unseen world is more real than the seen, for the world will one day pass away. Eternity is forever.

True faith transforms us and imparts courage. We can live with conviction and hope because our God is all-powerful and completely trustworthy.

—CYNTHIA HEALD
Becoming a Woman of Faith

Faith Is Action

I will love you, O LORD, my strength.
The LORD is my rock and my fortress and my deliverer;
My God, my strength, in whom I will trust.
I will call upon the LORD, who is worthy to be praised;
So shall I be saved from my enemies.

—PSALM 18:1–3

*B*ecause an idea or a dream starts in one's heart and mind, faith to believe in it cannot be based on outer circumstances; it must be based on God's inner work of confidence and direction— through His Word and Spirit—which will in turn provide visible "markers" as confirmation along the way.

Yet faith is not passive. It is an action, as is love. *To love* is to give, to accept, to sacrifice, to stand with, to believe in.

To have faith is to step in the direction toward what is believed to be the planned course of our lives. It is obeying God in the unseen areas of our lives. And because it is fueled by God alone, faith cannot develop without prayer and the Word. It is the consecutive string of thoughts, Scriptures, and promptings heard in the inner person, "Keep moving . . . turn here . . . stop briefly . . . knock on this door . . . step quickly," that propels us through the course of a dream, a project, or an idea.

But how can we obey if we haven't heard Him speak? Prayer and the Word whisper, call out, point, promise, and goad us in each and every step . . .

If we will only make time to listen.

Faith cannot be mustered up, engineered, or manipulated; it is a response from within us, orchestrated by God. It is a supernatural confidence inspired by a supernatural God.

—BECKY TIRABASSI
Let Faith Change Your Life

Keep Walking as Christ Walked

Therefore we also, since we are surrounded by so great a cloud of witnesses, let us lay aside every weight, and the sin which so easily ensnares us, and let us run with endurance the race that is set before us, looking unto Jesus, the author and finisher of our faith, who for the joy that was set before Him endured the cross, despising the shame, and has sat down at the right hand of the throne of God. For consider Him who endured such hostility from sinners against Himself, lest you become weary and discouraged in your souls.

—HEBREWS 12:1–3

*L*ife can be hard—and grossly unfair. When the bad things happen, we often ask, "Can I trust God?" But perhaps the real question is, "Can God trust me?" Can He trust us to hold on? Can He trust us to want to become mature Christians, or will we remain little children who believe in Him only if He makes it worth our while? When life seems to cave in for no reason at all, will we remember that God is faithful?

If we're going to be able to handle life when it doesn't seem to make sense, we have to get real. We have to set our faces in the right direction and keep walking as He walked. At times the road will be long and dark, the mountains unscalable. Because we're human we won't always make perfect choices. Sometime it will seem we take two steps forward and one step back, but it doesn't really matter. *All that really matters is being on the right road.*

—SHEILA WALSH
*Life Is Tough But God Is
Faithful*

Trusting God

Trust in the LORD with all your heart,
And lean not on your own understanding;
In all your ways acknowledge Him,
And He shall direct your paths.

—PROVERBS 3:5–6

Strong women intrigue me. I enjoy watching them organize large fund-raisers that make life better for less fortunate individuals. I admire parenting skills that strong women use; they work carefully to empower their children and help them grow strong. I enjoy observing strong women manage and make good business decisions. I envy their abilities to run companies and raise frisky families, all at the same time. The world is a good place because of sensitive, strong women.

But when is strength really a weakness? I have to admit that when it comes to the big decisions of life, trusting God is not my first line of thought. Instinctively I look within myself for answers. I am comfortable depending on my own resourcefulness. But the very foundation of a walk with God is complete trust. This kind of trust reflects the sense of security that comes from having Someone in whom to place total faith. This kind of trust calls for a total commitment of mind, purpose, and being. My strength must come from my faith in God, not the other way around. God is the only One who can keep my life straight and who can reveal the true and good will for my days. He does this for women who trust Him to lead.

How often I make my plans and ask for God's blessing on my plan. Then with jaw set I move ahead, thinking that my will is His will. Which finds me, again and again, needing to return to my point of departure and seek His wisdom on the front end of a decision—including Him in all of life.

Trusting God does not make me less of a woman; it doesn't compromise my personality as a strong woman. Depending on Him celebrates the wonderful, miraculous gift He has entrusted to me. Trusting Him *is* my strength.

—SUZANNE DALE EZELL
Living Simply in God's
Abundance

Faith Is Being Loved

It shall come to pass that before they call, I will answer;
And while they are still speaking, I will hear.

—ISAIAH 65:24

In this is love, not that we loved God, but that He loved us
and sent His Son to be *the propitation for our sins.*

—1 JOHN 4:10

A relevant faith lives within the framework that God is as real as our best friend or wisest counselor, *only* all-knowing, all-powerful, and always present. Once we believe that God is present in our lives, we can begin to live supernaturally in our environment, expecting that He will and can guide us by . . .

- giving us motivating thoughts, new ideas, and exciting dreams to pursue.

- instructing us through His written Word, the Bible.

- orchestrating events on our behalf.

- opening avenues of opportunity for us.

- directing us through another's timely advice.

When you are convinced that faith is more than an idea or "it," that it is being *loved* by Someone who can help, renew, empower, improve, forgive, and meet you in your darkest moments, it becomes the most relevant resource you have to change your life!

—BECKY TIRABASSI
Let Faith Change Your Life

Long Obedience

Not that I have already attained, or am already perfected; but I press on, that I may lay hold of that for which Christ Jesus has also laid hold of me. Brethren, I do not count myself to have apprehended; but one thing I do, forgetting those things which are behind and reaching forward to those things which are ahead, I press toward the goal for the prize of the upward call of God in Christ Jesus.

—PHILIPPIANS 3:12–14

*S*omeone once said that the challenge of living is to develop *a long obedience in the same direction.* When it's demanded, we can rise on occasion and be patient . . . as long as there are limits. But we balk when patience is required over a long haul. We don't much like endurance. It's painful to persevere through a marriage that's forever struggling. A church that never crests 100 members. Housekeeping routines that never vary from week-to-week. Even caring for an elderly parent or a handicapped child can feel like a long obedience in the same direction.

If only we could open our spiritual eyes to see the fields of grain we're planting, growing, and reaping along the way. That's what happens when we endure. Even the three decades I've lived in a wheelchair is, in a way, like driving on a long, straight road through miles and miles of cornfields—I have to keep reminding myself of the harvest of righteousness being produced in my life. "No discipline seems pleasant at the time, . . . later on, however, it produces a harvest of righteousness and peace for those who have been trained by it" (Heb. 12:11).

Right now you may be in the middle of a long stretch of the same old routine. The beginning of your Christian life was exhilarating. Your spiritual adrenaline was pumped up. But now there are miles behind you and miles to go. You don't hear any cheers or applause. The days run together—and so do the weeks. Your commitment to keep putting one foot in front of the other is starting to falter.

Take a moment and look at the fruit. *Perseverance. Determination. Fortitude. Patience.*

Your life is not a boring stretch of highway. It's a straight line to heaven. And just look at the fields ripening along the way. Look at the tenacity and endurance. Look at the grains of righteousness. You'll have quite a crop at harvest . . . so don't give up!

—JONI EARECKSON TADA
Holiness in Hidden Places

The Dailyness of Our Journey

Then He said to them all, "If anyone desires to come after Me, let him deny himself, and take up his cross daily, and follow Me. For whoever desires to save his life will lose it, but whoever loses his life for My sake will save it."

—LUKE 9:23–24

I wonder how often we postpone our walk with God until life seems a little more under control. "When I don't have to work so hard . . . when the children are in school . . . when my parents are better . . . when I have more time . . . *then* I will begin my journey." How tragic to go through life without realizing that our walk toward God's heart is a daily journey. We cannot make up for lost time. We can never recover yesterday.

Our walk with the Lord is a daily commitment to identify with Jesus.

Knowing this is freeing to me. I don't have to be perfect. I don't have to have all the spiritual disciplines in place. If I am willing to follow Christ, then each day becomes a time of preparation. Each day, no matter what it brings, is part of the process of my journey to God's heart.

Yet sometimes the very dailyness of this process can discourage us. We feel that we're not making any spiritual progress. We see no growth or ministry or significant service.

I remember a young mother of three boys asking me, "All I do is cook, clean, and go to soccer games—is that enough?" The answer is yes! Even though we do not sense that we are doing anything profound for God, it is important to understand that God continually works in the daily circumstances of our lives. Our part is not to look at our situation, but to set our hearts to draw near to our heavenly Father. Our circumstances should not dictate when we begin our journey.

—CYNTHIA HEALD
A Woman's Journey to the
Heart of God

Offering Up Yourself

Trust in the LORD, and do good;
Dwell in the land, and feed on His faithfulness.

—PSALM 37:3

For the LORD has heard the voice of my weeping.
The LORD has heard my supplication;
The LORD will receive my prayer.

—PSALM 6:8–9

*M*y theme is oblation—the offering up of ourselves, all we are, have, do, and suffer. Sacrifice means something received and something offered.

But some may be wondering, *How, exactly, do I do this?* I hesitate to prescribe a method for so solemn and vital a spiritual transaction. God knows your heart and will accept your offering in any way you can make it, I am sure, but a very simple thing has helped me. It is to kneel with open hands before the Lord. Be silent for a few minutes, putting yourself consciously in His presence. Think of Him. Then think of what you have received in the four categories mentioned (are, have, do, suffer)—the gift of a child, for example, or years later, the empty nest; the gift of work or the inability to work; marriage or singleness; pleasures or burdens; joy or sorrow. Next, visualize as well as you can this gift, resting there in your open hands. Thank the Lord for whatever aspect of this gift you can honestly thank Him for—if not for the thing in itself, then for its transformability, for His sovereignty, His will which allows you to have this gift, His unfailing love, the promise of His presence in deep waters and hot fires, the Pattern for Good which you know He is at work on. Then, quite simply, offer it up. Make God's gift to you your oblation to Him. Lift up your hands. This is a physical act denoting your love, your acceptance, your thanksgiving, and your trust that the Lord will make of it something redemptive for the wholeness of the Body, even for the life of the world.

I think you will begin to know the strange peace that is not the world's kind.

—ELISABETH ELLIOT
The Path of Loneliness

Constant Communication

The LORD will guide you continually,
And satisfy your soul in drought,
And strengthen your bones;
You shall be like a watered garden,
And like a spring of water, whose waters do not fail.

—ISAIAH 58:11

I often wonder why God wakes me up in the wee hours of the morning and puts ideas in my head. Is it because everybody else is asleep and He knows I won't be distracted? Is it because He knows that's the time I'm most receptive? It can't be because that's the time my name is called in His heavenly roll call. But invariably He'll wake me up between 3:00 and 5:00 A.M. . . .

God speaks to me in a variety of ways. Sometimes it's through dreams as I sleep and visions as I meditate. I can tell if it's God speaking to me because I can remember all the details of the dream or vision today as if I had just dreamed it.

Sometimes my left ear gets numb as He speaks in my mind.

Sometimes He speaks to me through Scripture.

Sometimes He speaks to me

- through the words of a song.

- through a reading or a sermon.

- through a quote or a prayer.

- through a word of advice or admonition.

- through the honesty of a child.

- from a billboard or a bumper sticker.

- through a conversation with a family member or friend.

But when He wakes me up in the wee hours of the morning, He has my complete and undivided attention.

When He speaks to me, He is never frightening.

He never tells me to do something that is harmful to myself or someone else.

He always tells me things that are in line with His Holy Word.

He does not always give me all the details.

His information is always correct.

When I follow His directions, I will make no mistakes.

He brings to pass everything He says.

I am amazed and humbled to realize that an awesome, omnipotent, sovereign God would want to communicate with me. But that's one of the reasons He created us: He wants us to have fellowship with Him. People have tried to explain how to hear the voice of God. In my opinion, nobody has been able to describe it fully. I believe God's sheep know the Shepherd's voice by faith.

If you want to hear whatever God has to say to you, simply ask. In the Lord's Prayer, these requests have to do with God's guidance in our lives:

- "Thy will be done in earth, as it is in heaven."

- "Lead us not into temptation, but deliver us from evil."

These requests alone open the door for God to personally communicate with us. Let us heed the voice of the Master.

—THELMA WELLS
What's Going On, Lord?

Partnering with God

. . . casting all your care upon Him, for He cares for you.

—1 PETER 5:7

From the end of the earth I will cry to You,
When my heart is overwhelmed;
Lead me to the rock that is higher than I.
For You have been a shelter for me . . .
I will trust in the shelter of Your wings.

—PSALM 61:1–4

*L*ife is filled with annoying little cheer depleters. I have often pondered how many of these little imperfections to bring to God's attention and how many to simply pass off. Will my cheer increase if I talk to God about the things that don't work?

For instance, does it make sense to ask God for a sunny day with no smog because Aunt Wilda is coming from Toronto, and I want it to be nice for her? Is it reasonable as I walk into the office supply store to ask God to help me find the fax machine paper that doesn't curl up like a scroll the minute it exits my machine? Does it make sense to pray that my newspaper be delivered a bit early so I can take it with me on my morning flight since I forgot to put it on vacation hold? To what degree is God involved in these daily issues? . . .

Not long ago I had lunch with Luci Swindoll and her brother Orville. He had come to California to install some new and complex computer equipment for Luci. As we were lunching, I gave my personal, as well as unsolicited, testimony about computers. That led to a discussion of prayer and the degree to which we pull God into our various small concerns. I asked Orville for his view.

He said, "You know, Marilyn, I pray about everything. Absolutely everything. For me, it is not so much the items I want Him to take note of as it is my desire to have unbroken communication with Him. I just want Him in on everything! Talking to Him causes me to sense our partnership."

The simple profundity of his comments caused this age-old issue finally to recede for me. I think one of my mental and spiritual hang-ups has been that, because of the fallout from the Fall, I've assumed I have to muck my own way through certain things; it's part of the package. I've never assumed God's indifference but have questioned my own need to use my head. Now I see the notion of bringing God into everything has nothing to do with trivializing Him; it has to do with the privilege of partnering with Him. When I include God . . . I'm cheered by His companionship and the knowledge that I'm in partnership with Him.

Why don't you give it a try? Today as you encounter things that don't work, include God in the aftermath of machinery gone haywire. It cheers me up just to think about that!

—MARILYN MEBERG
I'd Rather Be Laughing

Full-Time Speaking Terms

Then you shall call, and the LORD will answer;
You shall cry, and He will say,
'Here I am.'

—ISAIAH 55:9

I don't believe we're all called to a full-time ministry of inter-
cession, but I do believe we're all called to be on full-time speaking terms with the Lord God of the heavens. I find I stray if I
don't pray. It's just that simple. Without that personal connec-
tion and accountability, I lose my way. No wonder he calls us
sheep. No wonder we need a Shepherd.

We are told in the Gospel of John, "The sheep hear his voice,
and he calls his own sheep by name, and leads them out. When
he puts forth all his own, he goes before them, and the sheep follow him because they know his voice" (John 10:3–4).

No thrill matches hearing the Shepherd say our name, and
no joy touches the experience of hearing his voice as we follow.
I'm surprised we have to be reminded to talk to him . . . but I
do. *Baa.*

As I was writing this, the phone on my desk rang. My sister was calling from Florida to tell me our mom, an Alzheimer's patient, suddenly was having lucid moments. Would I like to talk to her?

I hadn't spoken with my mom for many months because she was incapable of understanding what a telephone was much less carry on a conversation.

Elizabeth wheeled Mom to the phone, and I heard my mother say, "Hello, who is this?"

My heart beat faster at the sound of her dear voice. A voice is such an intimate part of a person, and I found myself flooded with joy and loneliness all at the same time. I hadn't realized how much I had missed the warmth of her words. We talked for ten minutes, with me repeating myself over and over in an attempt to speak through her 80 percent hearing loss. I sang to her several of her favorite hymns, hoping she would remember them.

At one point I said, "Mom, I love you."

She heard that. "Oh, thank you, I love you, too. I haven't talked to you in a long time," she said matter-of-factly.

"Yes, Mom," I answered. "It's been far too long."

I wonder if the Lord doesn't speak to us over and over again in an attempt to converse through our deafness. Has it been a long time since you've talked with him? Far too long? I bet if we'd stop right now and listen, really listen, we'd hear him say, "I love you."

—PATSY CLAIRMONT

Mending Your Heart in a Broken World

A Focused Longing

By this My Father is glorified, that you bear much fruit; so you will be My disciples.

—JOHN 15:8

Let your light so shine before men, that they may see your good works and glorify your Father in heaven.

—MATTHEW 5:16

When our deepest desire is to bring God glory, then everything else in our lives is focused on this one longing. We become His true disciples, who want nothing more than to honor Him by bearing fruit for His praise.

One result of deep abiding, which produces much fruit, is that what we do will attract people not to us but to the Lord. The difference between the Pharisee and the true disciple is that the Pharisee serves in order to be noticed; the true disciple serves in order that God might be noticed. A true disciple is gentle, humble, unpretentious, sensitive, and gracious.

I have a friend who is a true disciple. When she sees a need, she doesn't say, "Let me know if I can help." She helps. I may find a plate of cookies on my porch or a special book we talked about. I receive notes of encouragement from her. When I'm involved in a project, she may call and say, "I'm bringing dinner for you this week—which night is best?" I find myself thanking the Lord for her. She does not bring glory to herself, because her serving is unobtrusive. I see her good works, but I give glory to God.

So how do you know if you are bringing glory to God? Whenever you do something selflessly, God receives glory. You please Him when you give in secret. You bless Him when you continually thank Him for His love, grace, goodness, sovereignty, and comfort. You glorify Him when you walk by faith and trust Him with all your heart. You show Him that you love Him when you choose to obey and abide.

—CYNTHIA HEALD
*A Woman's Journey to the
Heart of God*

Giving Him Glory

My heart is steadfast, O God, my heart is steadfast;
I will sing and give praise.

—PSALM 57:7

He has put the desire to worship deep within our hearts, and He wants us to raise our hearts and voices to Him. The word *praise* is recorded in the Bible *216* times (according to *Strong's Concordance of the Bible*); it must be pretty important! Psalm 22:3 says that God inhabits our praise. When we worship, He is in our midst. That's why there is such great pleasure in honoring God with our praise for all He is and does, for His great love for humankind.

In Zephaniah 3, the prophet painted a magnificent picture of this holy love. After God condemned the religious people of the land for their moral decay, His merciful nature shone forth. He promised to gather His true children, the ones who offered Him praise, and sustain them as He destroyed His enemies. He would restore their fortunes before their very eyes and give them back their joy. And God would respond to His people's praise with his own:

> The LORD your God is with you,
>
> He is mighty to save.
>
> He will take great delight in you,
>
> He will quiet you with His love,
>
> He will rejoice over you with singing. (Zeph. 3:17 NIV)

How awesome to know that almighty God rejoices over us when we praise Him!

It is *good* and *pleasant* to praise the Lord: good for Him, pleasant for us. Praise is a two-way street. Hallelujah!

—THELMA WELLS
What's Going On, Lord?

Acknowledgments

Grateful acknowledgment is made to the following publishers and copyright holders for permission to reprint copyrighted material:

Dee Brestin and Kathy Troccoli, *Falling in Love with Jesus,* 2000, W Publishing Group, Nashville, Tennessee. All rights reserved.

Patsy Clairmont, *I Love Being a Woman,* a Focus on the Family book published by Tyndale House. Copyright © 1999 by Patsy Clairmont. All rights reserved. International copyright secured. Used by permission.

—*Mending Your Heart in a Broken World* by Patsy Clairmont. Copyright © 2001 by Patsy Clairmont. By permission of Little, Brown and Company, (Inc.).

—*Sportin' a 'Tude,* a Focus on the Family book published by Tyndale House. Copyright © 1996 by Patsy Clairmont. All rights reserved. International copyright secured. Used by permission.

Suzan Johnson Cook, excerpted by permission of Thomas Nelson Publishers from the book entitled *Too Blessed to Be Stressed,* copyright date 1998 by Dr. Suzan Johnson Cook.

Harriet Crosby, excerpted by permission of Thomas Nelson Publishers from the book entitled *A Place Called Home,* copyright date 1997 by Harriet E. Crosby.

Elisabeth Elliot, *The Path of Loneliness*, © 1998 & 2001 by Elisabeth Elliot. Published by Servant Publications, P.O. Box 8617, Ann Arbor, Michigan, 48107. Used with permission.

Suzanne Dale Ezell, excerpted by permission of Thomas Nelson Publishers from the book entitled *Living Simply in God's Abundance,* copyright date 1998 by Suzanne Dale Ezell.

Cynthia Heald, excerpted by permission of Thomas Nelson Publishers from the book entitled *Becoming a Woman of Faith*, copyright date 2000 by Cynthia Heald.

—Excerpted by permission of Thomas Nelson Publishers from the book entitled *Becoming a Woman of Grace*, copyright date 1998 by Cynthia Heald.

—Excerpted by permission of Thomas Nelson Publishers from the book entitled *A Woman's Journey to the Heart of God*, copyright date 1997 by Cynthia Heald.

Liz Curtis Higgs, excerpted by permission of Thomas Nelson Publishers from the book entitled *Mirror, Mirror, on the Wall, Have I Got News for You!* copyright date 1997 by Liz Curtis Higgs.

—Excerpted by permission of Thomas Nelson Publishers from the book entitled *Only Angels Can Wing It, the Rest of Us Have to Practice,* copyright date 1995 by Liz Curtis Higgs.

Barbara Jenkins, excerpted by permission of Thomas Nelson Publishers from the book entitled *Wit and Wisdom for Women*, copyright date 1996 by Barbara Jenkins.

Barbara Johnson, *God's Most Precious Jewels Are Crystallized Tears;* 2001, W Publishing Group, Nashville, Tennessee.

—*I'm So Glad You Told Me What I Didn't Wanna Hear,* 1996, W Publishing Group, Nashville, Tennessee.

—*Mama, Get The Hammer, There's a Fly on Papa's Head,* 1994, W Publishing Group, Nashville, Tennessee.

—*Pack Up Your Gloomees in a Great Big Box Then Sit on the Lid and Laugh,* 1993, W Publishing Group, Nashville, Tennessee.

—*Splashes of Joy in the Cesspools of Life,* 1992, W Publishing Group, Nashville, Tennessee.

—*So, Stick a Geranium in Your Hat and Be Happy,* 1990, W Publishing Group, Nashville, Tennessee.

Nicole Johnson, excerpted by permission of Thomas Nelson Publishers from the book entitled *Fresh-Brewed Life,* copyright date 1999 by Nicole Johnson.

Marilyn Meberg, *Choosing the Amusing,* 1999, W Publishing Group, Nashville, Tennessee.

—*I'd Rather Be Laughing,* 1998, W Publishing Group, Nashville, Tennessee.

Miriam Neff, excerpted by permission of Thomas Nelson Publishers from the book entitled *Sisters of the Heart,* copyright date 1995 by Miriam Neff.

Stormie Omartian, excerpted by permission of Thomas Nelson Publishers from the book entitled *Finding Peace for Your Heart,* copyright date 1991 by Stormie Omartian.

—Excerpted by permission of Thomas Nelson Publishers from the book entitled *Lord, I Want to Be Whole,* copyright date 2000 by Stormie Omartian.

Luci Swindoll, *You Bring the Confetti, God Brings the Joy,* 1986, W Publishing Group, Nashville, Tennessee. All rights reserved.

Joni Eareckson Tada, *Holiness in Hidden Places.* Copyright 1999 by Joni Eareckson Tada. Used by permission of J. Countryman, a division of Thomas Nelson, Inc.

—Excerpted by permission of Thomas Nelson Publishers from the book entitled *Ordinary People, Extraordinary Faith,* copyright date 2001 by Joni Eareckson Tada.

Becky Tirabassi, excerpted by permission of Thomas Nelson Publishers from the book entitled *Let Prayer Change Your Life,* copyright date 1990, 1992, 2000 by Becky Tirabassi.

Kathy Troccoli, *Different Roads.* Copyright 1999 by Kathy Troccoli. Used by permission of J. Countryman, a division of Thomas Nelson, Inc.

Holly Wagner, excerpted by permission of Thomas Nelson Publishers from the book entitled *Dumb Things He Does, Dumb Things She Does,* copyright date 2002 by Holly Wagner.

Sheila Walsh, excerpted by permission of Thomas Nelson Publishers from the book entitled *Life Is Tough But God Is Faithful,* copyright date 1999 by Sheila Walsh.

—Excerpted by permission of Thomas Nelson Publishers from the book entitled *Unexpected Grace,* copyright date 2002 by Sheila Walsh.

Thelma Wells, excerpted by permission of Thomas Nelson Publishers from the book entitled *Girl, Have I Got Good News for You,* copyright date 2000 by Thelma Wells.

—Excerpted by permission of Thomas Nelson Publishers from the book entitled *God Will Make a Way,* copyright date 1998 by Thelma Wells.

—Excerpted by permission of Thomas Nelson Publishers from the book entitled *What's Going On, Lord?* copyright date 1999 by Thelma Wells.